R.C. Hutchinson

R.C. Hutchinson

The Man and his Writing

Barry Webb

The Lutterworth Press

THE LUTTERWORTH PRESS

P.O. Box 60
Cambridge
CB1 2NT
United Kingdom

www.lutterworth.com.
publishing@lutterworth.com

Hardback ISBN: 978 0 7188 9800 7
Paperback ISBN: 978 0 7188 9799 4
PDF ISBN: 978 0 7188 9802 1
ePub ISBN: 978 0 7188 9801 4

British Library Cataloguing in Publication Data
A record is available from the British Library

First published by The Lutterworth Press, 2024

This book is dedicated to the memory of the late Sir Rupert Hart-Davis and the late Peter Way, both of whom introduced me to the works of R.C.H.

'R.C. Hutchinson is not the first great writer who has had to wait for posthumous recognition and continued readership, and both, I am convinced, will come sooner or later...Genius is impossible to define, and the word has become tarnished by exposure, but I believe R.C. Hutchinson had it.'

– Sir Rupert Hart-Davis

'When someone – as someone surely will – comes to write about the total oeuvre of R.C. Hutchinson he will not find it easy to categorize the novels: each is different from its predecessors, all remain uninfluenced by contemporary fashion in fiction. His latest (Image of My Father) would break away from any pattern a critic was trying to impose... It is a quite remarkable novel.'

– Daniel George, *The Bookman*, September 1961

Contents

Acknowledgements

It was while I was teaching at Radley College in the 1980s that my colleague and friend Peter Way, who it appeared had read everything, introduced me to the novels of R.C.Hutchinson. I was immediately hooked and could not understand why nobody had written a proper assessment of his writing. I wondered if, perhaps, I might do so myself. But as so often, life seemed to intervene. The major but welcome intervention was finding myself becoming the biographer of the First World War veteran poet, scholar, teacher, biographer, essayist, Edmund Blunden – who I had met when I was an undergraduate and he was Oxford Professor of Poetry. This had an unexpected side-effect for it brought me in contact with Sir Rupert Hart-Davis, a life-long friend of Blunden and his unofficial literary trustee. This resulted in several visits to Marske-in-Swaledale. I found myself in the presence once again of someone who had apparently read everything and when I asked him about R.C.Hutchinson he was fulsome with praise for his writing, showed me signed copies of all the novels and explained that he always wanted to be his publisher.

This volume is dedicated to both these early inspirers of my reading of Hutchinson.

Eventually, in retirement, I found myself in the position of being able to embark on the project I had wanted to pursue some forty years earlier. Not knowing whether there were any surviving close members of the family I discovered that his grandson was living in Oxford, being the Regius Professor of Greek, and very keen on the prospect of resurrecting the literary reputation of his grandfather. It also led to meeting all of Hutchinson's four children who were waiting for someone to bring their father to greater critical attention.

My research into bibliographical and biographical material was made immeasurably easier by being given free access to two large chests full of such papers and manuscripts. I cannot be more grateful to R.C.H.'s elder daughter Ann, guardian of this treasure trove, who gave me unhindered access over many visits to her London home. I was reassured to hear of her nodding in approval (though with occasional raising of the eyebrows) when the early draft of the opening chapters was read to her shortly before her death. Her sister, Elspeth, took over possession of the archive and continued to give me welcoming access. R.C.H.'s elder son, Jeremy, has been a great support from the start and has answered all enquiries with prompt and knowledgeable responses. I am also grateful to Piers, R.C.H.'s younger son, for a valuable conversation on a visit from Canada.

Robert Greene's masterly bibliography has been a constant reference companion. Both the bibliography and the family archive have saved me visits to the Harry Ransom Center at Texas (which would have been impossible during Covid) and I acknowledge the help given by Courtney Welu and Cathy Henderson at the library in producing illustrations and extracts from R.C.H.'s schoolboy diary and novel.

I remember a valuable conversation with R.C.H.'s friend the late Charles Wrinch right at the earliest days of considering this project. Similarly, conversations with the late Sir Patrick Nairne, a fellow enthusiastic reader of R.C.H.

For help with information about R.C.H.'s schooldays I am indebted to Peter LeRoy and to the archivists at Monkton Combe School, Caroline Bone and Jacqueline Burrows.

Bishop Richard Harries was an early encourager for writing this volume and has continued to be so until its conclusion. Thanks are also due to the late Jonty Driver and to Canon Professor Nigel Biggar. I am also grateful for a conversation with the cellist Steven Isserlis who had read every novel of R.C.H. I also thank Sebastian Faulks for permission to quote his admiration for the work of R.C.H.

For financial help throughout the publishing process I offer my thanks to Felicity and Chris Kershaw and Penelope Warner, and especially to Victor Glynn who has been a source of encouragement from first to last. William Arthur has been endlessly patient as a technological assistant transferring my erratic typescript into readable computer format – and adding several acute observations on content. Max Tucker has also come to the rescue at moments of computer panic.

Richard Smail has been a friend and supporter in every way – reading each early draft with meticulous care and a sensitive ear for which I am most grateful.

Lutterworth Press could not have been more supportive and efficient. I am grateful for the belief in the project shown by Adrian Brink and by my tireless editor Sarah Algar-Hughes. Thanks are due to Georgina Melia who designed the cover and to Ana Almeida at Sales and Publicity. It has been a pleasure to work with such a professional and friendly team.

Copyright Acknowledgements

Prologue

By 1976, R.C. Hutchinson was an acclaimed novelist, winner of the *Sunday Times* 'Gold Medal for Fiction' for his novel *Testament*, winner of the W.H. Smith Award for his novel *A Child Possessed* and shortlisted for the Booker Prize for his final novel *Rising*. At his death he had published seventeen novels, including *The Unforgotten Prisoner* – which achieved 150,000 sales in its first month. He was highly regarded by many of his contemporary writers, including Stephen Spender and Cecil Day Lewis. Fifty years later he has become an almost forgotten figure, mostly out of print, though he has always had his enthusiastic followers such as the novelist Sebastian Faulks, the theologian and writer Bishop Richard Harries, and the acclaimed cellist Steven Isserlis.

Hutchinson claimed in a remarkable schoolboy diary (written at the age of 15, and reading like a draft of a mature autobiography) that 'I have decided to write a diary of thought, since my life consists, I think, more in thought than in deed.' Certainly his personal life was to be predominantly a private one, devoid of scandal, centred on a happy marriage and family life, and lived more in the seclusion of his library than in the literary world, which held little appeal to him, partly from an innate shyness. His writings will not evoke the literary or social life of his times, and he never followed the changing tastes of the novel-reading public. The novels, however, offer an extraordinary vision of the world of Europe before and after the Second World War (a vision in part influenced by his own unusual war experience), and concentrate on the effects of war on its survivors.

Most remarkable is his ability to write with exceptionable authenticity about places he had never visited. This imaginative ability extends to an acute understanding and sympathy with the internal sufferings of his characters: as one acute critic observed, he takes his readers 'along some private avenue where nobody walks but he' and another describes his 'penetrative eye which drives into the odd corners of the soul'. His vision that the answer to human suffering lies in his own belief in the power of divine intervention is a constant theme throughout his work, though his characters are never just mere puppets. The characters are instead sympathetically seen as striving for some sense of release from their individual spiritual journeys. All this is tempered occasionally with a highly individual strand of humour, sometimes dark, sometimes highly comic.

One loyal publisher, Peter Day, who reissued three of Hutchinson's novels, explained his aim in rescuing 'forgotten' authors:

> What is it that makes us pick up and read a book again and again? The memory of that first immersion when everything but what we were reading pales into insignificance? When the book ate with us, walked with us, travelled with us, slept with us, and, when it was finished, we grieved as for the loss of a close friend ... There comes a time when we realise that we haven't seen it let alone read it for years, and when we try to get it in the bookshop find that it is out of print and there are no plans to reprint ... these are my favourites, books I think should be in print, books I really believe you will want to read and enjoy, books that will speak to you as they have to me.

These wise words encapsulate the intention of this volume, in offering the works of Ray Coryton Hutchinson to a new readership. The story begins in a delightful Somerset valley, where the teenage Hutchinson was writing his private diary, which he referred to as his 'red book'.

Chapter 1

Monkton Combe and Childhood

The village of Monkton Combe is situated on the south-facing slope of a tree-lined hill, overlooking the picturesque valley of Limpley Stoke, three miles from the city of Bath, Somerset. In medieval times the monks of Bath Abbey farmed this 'cume' (or 'hollow'), hence its name. The village is an isolated hamlet, approached by narrow winding lanes, and consists mostly of a curving main street with simple cottages and houses focusing on Midford Brook along the bottom of the valley. In 1868 a remarkable vicar of Monkton Combe, the Reverend Francis Pocock, who had rebuilt the church and designed a new vicarage, founded a school to uphold the evangelical traditions of the Anglican Church. Monkton Combe was to become a leading influence among a small group of independent schools dedicated to foster this ideal, both within the educational sphere and in public life. By 1922 it was firmly established and it was where the 15-year-old Ray Hutchinson was beginnig to record his thoughts, impressions and hopes in his schoolboy diary.

The choice of school was no accident, for his parents were evangelical to an almost fanatical degree. His father, Harry, had married Catherine Painter in 1901. She died thirteen months later, after giving birth to a son, Sheldon. Three years later Harry married Lucy Mabel Coryton, from a mixed Cornish and strongly Irish background. In 1907 she gave birth to a son, naming him Raymond Coryton. Mabel was convinced of the truth of the evangelical Christian tradition, the literal infallibility of the Bible (in the Authorised Version) and the possible imminence of 'the second coming' of Christ. To be ready for this she wore fresh underwear to bed every night in case the Almighty made a return in the small hours. She feared Roman Catholicism and would cross the road if she saw a nun approaching. Her personal copy of the Bible is annotated on nearly every page. She finds evidence that all non-Christian faiths are undermined by scriptural evidence. In particular she dismisses Darwinism on the interpretation of the genealogy of Jesus as laid down in the third chapter of the Gospel of Luke, which records a direct descent from Adam: 'Thus destroying Darwinism. No Evolution.' Similar evidence is found to dismiss Christian Science and any other non-evangelical Protestant denomination. These convictions were also evident on Harry's side of the family. His father, Henry, held meetings in his home with a prominent evangelical preacher, Josiah Spiers, who was dedicated to spreading the gospel among young people. In 1867 fifteen children attended a gathering in Henry's home in Islington, which became the cradle from which was formed the Children's Special Service Mission (later The Scripture Union) which held Christian services for young people on the beaches of Britain in the summer months. After severe personal financial business difficulties, Henry became the first secretary of the CSSM. This was the somewhat stringent religious atmosphere dominating the Hutchinsons' house in Finchley, London, which was to be Ray's home until he left Oxford.

It was a happy and close-knit family and Ray's early letters from school were affectionately addressed to 'Dear Pater' and 'Dear Mumzie' and in his diary he wrote that '"Mother"' I think should *always* be spelt with a capital'. As an adult he declared that he had been 'spoilt' as a child. He also remembered with pleasure being read, in the nursery, the works of Amy Le Feuvre – his first experience of literary enjoyment. But his reaction to the evangelicalism of his childhood upbringing was to have a profound and often conflicting impact on his later imaginative world.

His first educational steps took him to Hendon Preparatory School. Here signs of his talent and enthusiasm for reading and writing were quickly apparent. His termly reports consistently listed 'excellent' in the English column and he left with a scholarship to Tenterden Preparatory School in Hendon. The major event of his Tenterden days was his entry for an essay prize on 'War Models', an exhibition (mostly of tanks) displayed in London to raise money for disabled soldiers. The competition was open to all boys up to 18 years old. Harry and Mabel were the proud parents in the audience when Lady Haig, wife of the prominent First War general, handed the winning prize of two guineas to the 10-year-old Ray, commenting that his essay 'showed more originality and imagination than the efforts of the older boys'. Three years later Ray was wearing the uniform of a new boy at Monkton Combe.

He was always known as Ray to his family and friends, though some close friends also knew him as 'Hutch'. Except for his first novel he published as R.C. Hutchinson, but he was often referred to simply as R.C.H.

He was a good-looking teenager but there were some health worries as he was found to have a weak heart which threatened to curtail his sporting activities. His major athletic interest was rowing and Monkton Combe was strong on the river (it has produced an impressive list of Olympic medallists). He also played rugby to a competent level and enjoyed tennis. He was subject to constant medical examinations but managed to be given a clean bill of health for sport throughout his school career. He enjoyed the physical challenges of both rowing and rugby (he writes quite poetically of the sound of the oars driving through the water in a rowing race) but was scornful of 'people taking games in earnest' and of the ethos of 'muscular Christianity' which flourished as part of the idealism of religious education in Victorian England and extended into the 1920s. In later years he suggested his dislike of school rugby, but it seems it was more his description of the 'incessant' amount of rugby, its compulsory requirement and the assumption that it instilled moral virtue which irritated him, rather than the game itself.

Few statements could be more self-perceptive than the opening sentence of his schoolboy diary, (which he referred to as his 'red book'), declaring that he had 'decided to write a diary of thought, since my life consists, I think, more in thought than in deed'. Hutchinson's later years were not going to be full of incident – his personal life was to be, for the most part, one of happiness and married contentment; his war experience one of administrative skill and influence rather than physical challenge or suffering. Mostly from the privacy of his study his world view would be a predominately private one, a vivid and imaginative landscape which few of his contemporary writers would rival. By the age of 16 he was writing his internal autobiography. Future years would see this vision subtly and widely extended, but all the essential ingredients were already being recorded in his own hand in 1923. The diary opens with all the theatricality one would expect from a lively 16 year old. The title page includes the warning: 'In the case of the owner's death to be DESTROYED IMMEDIATELY', and adds the note: 'This diary contains matter of the UTMOST PRIVACY. It is therefore requested that no one but the owner read or glance through its pages.'

By far the most common subject for discussion in its pages is religion, and there are at least 70 entries covering his concerns, some of them at considerable length. Doubtless many adolescents are exercised by religious dilemmas and are confused as they move from one idea to another, but in Ray's case he seems to be writing a daily record of his theological journey and shows surprising maturity in the expression of this process. He confronts the problems of predestination, the possible 'state' of heaven, the problems of pain and suffering, temptation, the resurrection, providence, confession, celibacy, the relationship between the Old Testament and the New Testament, and the nature of divine inspiration in terms of biblical authorship. But his main preoccupation is how evangelicalism impinges on his home and school life and he frequently repeats his conviction that it strangles 'joy'. He shared this view with the figure who was his 'confessor' and his closest ally – his step-brother Sheldon: 'he is more than a friend, and more than a brother; to me he is everything'. Sheldon was some four years Ray's senior, an Old Monktonian who left for Cambridge just as Ray was starting his diary and who corresponded with Ray on a regular basis. Sheldon became an Anglo-Catholic priest, remembered as a larger-than-life character, a jovial and charitable parish clergyman (who would rather liked to have become a bishop). Ray could express himself freely and openly to him:

> I begin to feel more and more that Sheldon is everything to me. He has such a wonderful, perpetual sense of humour, coupled with such deep sympathy over everything; he is so broad-minded, he has both Faith and Humility – things I know only by name ... Sheldon's religion is a far, far finer thing than mine; he has joy, joy, joy brimming over... Talking of sympathy, I wish Christian people would learn it. Love is the whole thing in this bloody world; the Bible say so and it's right ... Love is the creative force in this world, but it is *more*, it is everything – *GOD* is love ... sympathy is really nothing but love, and love is everything.

He concludes one paragraph with the rather brutal observation: 'Monkton is just the same. There is no love in its religion.'

If he objected to what he saw as the lack of 'love' and 'joy' in the religious diet he was being offered, he was also suspicious of what he saw as false enthusiasm in its forms of worship. He attended (against his will) meetings arranged by the Crusaders – a youth group formed to encourage teenage boys (especially from public schools) towards the evangelical position. Ray records:

> This afternoon I was at the Crusaders as usual. How I hate it nowadays. This idea of 'religion served up in a palatable form' bores me to tears. The Crusader 'services' are so blatant and noisy. Boys are supposed to be fond of that sort of thing; perhaps some are; but I really believe that a quiet devotional service would appeal just as much to most of them. (That is what Sheldon says, and I agree with him). The choruses are horribly unpoetical and unmusical. The 'straight-forward' talks are stereotyped and lifeless. It is what people call the 'bright meeting'.

Such irritation is often balanced by a whimsical comic touch (and a mixture of humour and seriousness was to be a hallmark of his later narrative style):

> Really our Church-Worship is an extraordinary thing. I find it difficult to imagine the Almighty sitting up in Heaven with a smile on his face, listening to a lot of weary schoolboys moaning out the 'Venite' to the wheezy strains of the dissonant harmonium. This is what is known as 'praise'.

Having such convictions, and linked with the influence of Sheldon, it was not surprising that he was drawn in some respects to the High Church tradition but didn't want to distress his parents. They would doubtless have been somewhat alarmed if they had read his entry: 'the Eucharist without the idea of transubstantiation is, in my opinion, void. Why should we be afraid of that glorious mystery?'

But more important to Ray was his belief that evangelical enthusiasm was not giving his father 'joy' but making him unhappy. He was very conscious of Harry's difficult life: becoming a young widower, confronted with financial burdens, sacrificing much to see Ray through Monkton:

> Gad! What a life he has had ... Rotten home – parents
> stiff as starch and damnably evangelical. Love apparently
> of a formalised and conventional type. Marriage for one
> year, then, a son – and no wife. Then a second marriage;
> cussedness of first wife's relatives; no wonder his religion
> is of a joyless stereotyped evangelical sort of thing. Poor
> Father ... I owe everything to the pater.... I realise what a
> wonderful man he is ... I *must* give him some happiness.
> I must make love an *active* thing. I *must* not let my love
> grow cold. I must *conquer* him with love.

He continues: 'I think one day, if ever I am so energetic, I shall write a novel on the parent problem. How love remains, but opinions are yet so widely different. It is a problem.' He defines the 'problem' further:

> parents are the most priceless people going. With them
> it is all love, love, love; showers of it – but *no* knowledge.
> And they study me ... they tell me what 'stages' I am
> getting to ... it is rather topping to watch them studying:
> they know so little, and think they know so much.

Was the memory of his father's 'problems' part of the imaginative seed which inspired Ray's novel *Image of My Father*, written some 40 years later?

A comparable pattern can be seen in the relationship with his mother. There was no lack of affection, but an immense sense of frustration stemming from her religious enthusiasm: 'A most awful letter from home yesterday. Nothing but Bible truths etc., *I am* so tired of it.' He records reading the writings of Augusta Cook, a popular evangelical author of the time and a favourite of his Mother's. Presumably Mabel had been reading such volumes as *Light from the Book of Daniel on Past, Present and Future* and *The Divine Calendar: Vol.One: The Seven Seals. Vol.Two: The Seven Trumpets*. Ray was dismissive of Cook's writings:

> *Really* such fanaticism is something amazing. As works of
> humour, hers are the acme of perfection, but as anything

else, as religion, oh! Roman Anti-Christ, British-Israel, all the trimmings! The whole thing reeks of *blind* lunacy. Facts and figures twisted about and mixed up with odd texts from the Bible.

But he was very sympathetic to his mother's loyal support of his father and her constant efforts to be a good stepmother to Sheldon. Was the memory of his mother not part of the imaginative seed which inspired Ray's novel *The Stepmother*, written some 30 years later?

But there were other things to occupy a teenager's thoughts. For one thing he was strongly attracted to his younger step-cousin Esmé, who was a regular visitor to the Hutchinson home.

Topping kid; gad she will be a topping girl in a few years time; just at present I can do anything I like – kiss her when I want to – but in 1930? I wonder … There is no getting away from the fact, I am absolutely in love with Esmé. But love at my age never comes to anything.

He was also fascinated by the theatre and cinema: 'everyone should go *sometimes* to *good* films … the cinema is the thing of the day. It is everyone's *duty* to go to it.' He airs a rather prim view that the cinema can have the effect of showing the dire results of immoral behaviour, but this is countered by a more humane confession: 'Sin is very, *very* attractive!' There were other attractions to be gained from theatre visits apart from dramatic pleasure:

the worst of it is I always fall in love with the actresses on the spot. This afternoon there was a delightful little dancer there … I simply loved her at once. Incidentally she hardly wore anything. Yes, I am afraid I get a good deal of enjoyment from those dancing girls.

In an interesting footnote to an entry on the cinema he adds: 'I wonder if I could write scenarios?'

He also mentions his pleasure in smoking and the freedom of doing so at home, with easier evasions than the restrictions of school rules: 'Well, less than three weeks more, and I shall be having my first fag after eleven weeks. Oh my God, is there anything to be compared with the joy of that first fag?' As an adult he was rarely to be seen without his pipe, until in the last few years he was advised to give it up by his doctor.

There were intellectual avenues to explore too. He became a keen contributor to the school debating society which enabled him to express his views on, among other topics, euthanasia, vivisection, Tutankhamen, blood sports, and inter-racial marriage. The predominant political issue on his mind was the attraction of socialism. A very early entry in the diary describes an event which made a vivid impression on him and may have been a significant inspiration for his social and political explorations. He describes going for a walk in London in the New Year:

> In Haymarket I saw a little old man, who was lame, and haggard; everyone else was saying 'A happy new year'; *He* wasn't. He seemed to have no hope. Gad, what must life without all hope be like. Absolutely upset me, seeing that poor man. I could have wept on the spot; but as it was I got on a bus and went home, and had a damn good tea. That is what one calls sympathy; part and parcel of this damn world.

The figure of a crippled beggar appears in various representations throughout Hutchinson's novels.

He was keen to take a leading part in a debate on the French Revolution representing 'the supreme goal of the social tendencies of the present day' but the most forceful statements of socialist principles are combined in two entries:

> I am getting more and more convinced about socialism. You know we *must* give everyone a chance. They are not like ourselves, but they are made in our likeness. *Why* are *we* what we are? Is it from our brains, our superior characters? No, it is from our birth. And that is grossly unfair. It means that we have had a chance which the rest have not. That filthy little urchin in the gutter, why do I look down on him as a lower being? Has he done anything wrong? Has he less brains than I? No! But his father was born in a lower position than my father, hence … Oh it is pitiful, it is *grossly* unchristian … Yes the class system must go; it is mucking everything.

Academic matters also had to be fitted into his busy life. His interests in the classroom centred on literature and languages (his writings are full of characters speaking in colloquial French, German, and Spanish and are scattered with Latin quotations). Outside the classroom he was becoming a more than competent artist – mostly ink sketches – and developing an ear for classical music. His real passion, however, was concentrated on his reading. Considering that his diary only covers seven months it is remarkable that he makes references to Shakespeare, ('I cannot, and never shall, get over Shakespeare ... there never will be such a master of human thought and passion ... In Shakespeare drama reached the very height and summit of its possibilities') and Swift, Fielding, Boswell, Austen, Hardy, Victor Hugo, Corneille, Cervantes, Descartes, and Pascal (whose objective perspective on Christianity he found most appealing). He also read Balzac's *Poor Relations* (presumably Part One) within a week; Balzac was a novelist with whom R.C.H. was often to be compared. Dominating his literary interest, however, seems to have been Dickens. His fascination had an interesting origin. It was when he was in preparatory school that Ray heard a talk from a colourful Dickens disciple: The Reverend A.R. Runnels-Moss, for 23 years vicar of St John's, Ladywood, Birmingham, who was much in demand for his theatrical recitations of Dickens (especially extracts from *David Copperfield*). Ray was deeply impressed by his evocation of Pickwick, and his pleasure was further extended by another school visit when Runnels-Moss gave a repeat performance based on *A Tale of Two Cities*. Ray described the event in a letter to his mother as 'the jolliest day so far this term'. Runnels-Moss paid a third visit (this time to Monkton) when he spoke on *Don Quixote*. Ray records: 'It is a great and strange allegory that book, born in the prison, which pictures the idealist, and his fate; the man who sets out to "right the wrong". It is a remarkable blending of light and shade.'

In further diary entries, when he was going through a period of experimental agnosticism, he found particular comfort in some lines of Landor:

> *I strive with none, for none was worth my strife,*
> *Nature I loved, and next to Nature, Art.*
> *I warmed both hands before the fire of life,*
> *It sinks, and I am ready to depart.*

> I would give something to have written that; but it is no
> good, I shall never be a poet; it comes on me by fits and
> starts, but even then I never produce good work.

He did, however, experiment with writing poetry, even if his
instinct that it wasn't his natural talent proved correct. He began an
ambitious scheme for a five-part dramatic work on Judas Iscariot.
Only two parts survive in manuscript, consisting of passages of
pentameters with elusive rhyme schemes, interspersed with chorus-
like interludes on a classical model. The significant factor is the
choice of subject matter: guilt and betrayal, two aspects often to be
explored (particularly in a military context) in his novels, and he
later wrote a short story (unpublished) entitled 'Judas Iscariot'. The
surviving passages of his poem show some sophisticated control of
rhythmical patterns and some memorable poetical moments, but his
own analysis of his poetic powers seems accurate. He offered a poem,
as a sixth-former, to *The Monktonian* but there is no certain evidence
that it was published. He rather resented his lack of poetic skill: 'I
do know and feel poetry, and poetry: c'est toute la vie.' In 1962 he
contributed a brief introduction to an anthology of verse from Old
Monktonians, entitled *The Valley*. The poems are all anonymous, but
he suggests some might have special appeal for a variety of reasons,
indicating them by page references. But he also refers to 'a slab of
verse included here which strikes me as so execrable that I shall
give it no reference!' He can only be referring to his own verse, but
as they are anonymous, any published poems of his own remain
unidentifiable.

He was far more confident that his literary skills were likely to
flourish within the novel form, even if he was nervous about the
possibilities:

> Possibly I could write; I feel that I have materials for a best-
> seller, but my style would never go down ... I want to fill
> this book as much as possible with the various ideas that
> come into my head. Then I will have something to draw on
> for novels, etc., *IF* I ever write any ... somehow thoughts
> don't go well into writing, and vice versa. Probably the
> writer is at fault. It is *absurd* of me to imagine that I have
> any literary talent.

Nonetheless he found time to write, aged 15, a 20,000-word novel with the rather lurid title 'The Hand of the Purple Idol'. It is an intriguing piece of writing, following the traditions of the Victorian Gothic novel, starting in Italy (recounting previous events in remote Africa), before moving to wilder parts of England. It concerns the mysterious history of a curse which brings death to those who touch the hand of the purple idol, and the story involves shipwrecks, castles, disguises, and chance encounters. But it is more than a childish extravaganza. At times it reads as though Sherlock Holmes is reciting a tale to Dr Watson in 221B Baker Street, and indeed, Sherlock Holmes is referred to in the novel. There are moments of powerful description, particularly in the opening paragraphs of each chapter, and some mature observations of human character: 'What is more delightful than giving someone a pleasant surprise. From the earliest days every man has this desire in his heart.' And how many teenagers would open a story with an explanation of the title by reference to a quotation from Gibbon: 'A head to contrive and a hand to execute.' There are also sophisticated allusions in the chapter headings, including epigrams form Cicero ('Dum Spiro Spero'), quotations from Kipling and reference (presumably from his biblical knowledge) to an 'old man from Ascalon'. He also shows his future obsession with revisions to his texts, for there are numerous marginal suggestions of alterations and there is a correction in the first line of the narrative. The work only exists in manuscript and was later dismissed by R.C.H. as a juvenile thriller of no literary merit, but how many young teenagers have completed a novel, of whatever quality, while still at school?

Some of the comments in the 'red book' may well give the impression of a boy who would not recall his schooldays with very much affection, but it is a record of the private thoughts of a mid-teenager in his formative and most questioning years. There was much he enjoyed, including his rowing, and he made some life-long friendships – especially with Jeremy Churchill, a future doctor who became godfather to R.C.H.'s elder son, Jeremy, and A.K. Mathews, later Dean of St Albans. He also had great respect for his headmaster, the Reverend J.W. Kearns (always known as 'The Crow' because of his hooked nose). In many ways he became a faithful Old Monktonian, although it has taken nearly 100 years for Monkton to begin to return the compliment. He attended Old Boys' dinners and Old Boys' days, often writing entertaining reports of the events for the school magazine.

R.C.H. wrote a warm review of an eccentric Monkton master, A.F. Lace, who had written an autobiography entitled, *My Own Trumpet.*

R.C.H. called the review 'Schoolmaster Extraordinary'. He recalls Lace as a modest and hard-working man who 'did practically everything but scrub the floors and released for an hour or two on Saturday afternoons he played first-class rugby ... for fun!' Revealingly, the qualities that R.C.H. stresses as most admirable are hard work and geniality: 'He liked his colleagues. He liked boys. He liked teaching himself to teach. He thought it a natural condition of human life to be on duty twenty-four hours a day.' Amusingly he observes 'his ferocious castigation of those who use "so" as a conjunction sent me running, white-faced, to another distinguished schoolmaster, H.W. Fowler' (author of the acclaimed authority on grammar, *Modern English Usage)*, 'and although Fowler seemed to be on my side I was not entirely happy until, on two pages, I found A.F.L. quietly breaking his own rule'. As a footnote to the published article Lace added: 'Clearly my reviewer and I differ about conjunctions. *So* I have asked him to give me a lesson.' But perhaps the most pertinent sentence in the review is R.C.H. recalling his own memory of the school before 50 years had mellowed his view: 'when, arriving in "the delectable valley" some fifty years ago, I was tempted to think Monkton the most comfortless habitation so far devised by the ingenuity of man'.

He also contributed a warm obituary of his old French master, G.W.F.R. Goodridge, confined to a wheelchair 'but how very far from lame in spirit!' Goodridge asserted a magisterial and formidable presence and was a widely read scholar. R.C.H. noted shrewdly some of the qualities which contribute to good teaching:

> He was, I suppose more mimicked than any other master. The schoolmaster who is not mimicked has probably too colourless a personality to be suited to his job; he had better try a less subtle profession ... he had dignity; but he was by no means a portentously solemn man... That helps to explain how he could be so good – and permanent – a friend and therefore so very good a schoolmaster: in art and in life he understood both the magnificent and the ludicrous.

He would return his pupils' translations with curt phrases of reticent praise. R.C.H. remembered: 'This is yours H. This just won't do!' It would be a year later that he received the awaited praise: 'On the whole, this is quite a happy effort, H.' The obituary ends:

So short a note as this is unworthy of his size and genius; it fails to recall the flavour of his rare personality. But to those who knew him that will not need to be recalled. And he himself, reading this and knowing what the intention was, might say in his kindly, judicial way: 'This is yours, H. This is a little better.'

He also wrote at least three lengthy reports on Old Monktonian dinners, full of wry and vivid descriptions of such ritualistic events:

There was the same simmer and bubble of reminiscence, the same search for familiar features behind those strange moustaches with which the male asserts his individuality in competition with the infinite diversity of the female hat ... As usual the Church was thickly represented, and so was the medical profession. (It was remarked that a shout of 'motor accident outside!' would have cleared half the room in ten seconds; while the other half could have been emptied by a sharp cry of 'Fag!') ... It was pleasant to look back ... 'Those were the days!' we told each other splendidly; and thought of getting into chilly, mud-flaked shorts and imagined the desolation of the old pavilion ... and through the mists of time we dreamed of 'the happiest days of my life!' and to the waiter, sotto voce, we said, 'The same again!'

He captures with comic precision the inevitable humour of trying to recognize one's contemporaries, no longer in sports kit but in smart evening dress; no longer thin, nervous adolescents but overweight, be-whiskered confident professional men. More than once he asks that speeches be shortened so that there is more time for the 'main business of the evening' without the threat of missing the last train home. The 'main business' being the broken tides of talk flowing between the tables:

'Extraordinary thing – I ran into him in Bangkok' ... 'He was with the Gunners in the Anzio party' ... 'No, but I married three of his sisters in Tasmania' ... 'I took out his tonsils at Cape Town but it didn't work so I put them back at Karachi!' ... 'before your time. I remember the Duke

saying to me, just after Vimiero' ... 'Well, you *will* look me
up whenever you're in Puerto Rico?'. So that for some of us,
in this brief hour, both time and space seem to have fallen
asleep; while a hundred miles away, in the valley which had
first brought us all together, the young barbarians (if they
are as virtuous as we were) also slept.

Another recollection ended, 'It was, however, a tumultuously
joyful evening... "We believe," said the Headmaster, "That the Lord
will build this house and therefore we labour not in vain that build it."
We felt that this was no shallow utterance.'

The most memorable and lively description, however, was the
lengthy record of the Old Boys' Day 1937:

> The great philosopher, P.G. Woodhouse refers to Old
> Boys' functions in some such terms as these: 'You want to
> avoid that kind of thing, Cheddars. You only find yourself
> jammed tight between two centenarians who sprawl in
> front of you until their beards are touching and jabber to
> each other in cracked voices about how they were given
> an extra half-holiday to celebrate the battle of Crecy.' But
> Mr. Woodhouse is wrong, for on Old Boys' Day age and
> time are thrown into such confusion that the difference
> between the Real Old Boy and the New Old Boy seems
> to flicker and fade ... and Monkton's aspect adds to the
> confusion ... It is at once disconcerting and delightful:
> you are humiliated when you lose your way, you sniff with
> a certain relish the consecrated odour of the unalterable
> boot-room, you catch your breath with pleasure when the
> beauty of the new buildings breaks so unexpectedly into
> your vision. How lovely Longmead looked that day, with the
> new pavilion fitting as comfortably between the chestnuts
> as if it had always stood there, What an incomparable field
> it is, and especially when ... behind the gay rim of frocks
> and blazers there is a towering cloud of such green as
> cannot be matched in all the West Country ...At luncheon
> we sat almost shyly in the splendour of the new hall, eating
> the finest strawberry tarts that were ever concocted, with
> lashes of cream ... More cricket, and ever so much more

food; the delicious melodies of 'Merrie England,' and then, next morning, the excitement of the Eight's departure in high courage for Henley ... A spell of memories, not least the quieter memory of early morning, when three headmasters gathered us again in the fellowship of Holy Communion. There we realized most deeply and gratefully that Monkton is, and always will be, a great family.

Such were R.C.H.'s later feelings and reflections, but to return to the 'red book', two final entries summarise the conflicting feelings that any school leaver has, looking back and thinking of the future. One is a searing self-appraisal and reflection on his school life:

> I have been thinking rather of the practical advantages one gets from the public-school career; it strikes me this way: I am a blundering fool. I forget things and am generally thoughtless. I am shy and fiddling – can never be at ease with people I don't know. In the intellectual department I am grossly unpractical; there are hundreds round about me who have not had my educational advantages – and they are practical; they don't forget things, they are straightforward, and know the ropes; not so adaptable perhaps, but infinitely more – well practical, there is no other term for it. But if it came really to a crisis, if we came up against the core of things, I flatter myself I would have it; because I am not afraid of a little hell; THEY don't know what it is like to get in front of an opposing scrum and drop on the bloody ball; THEY don't know, moreover, what it is to face that shrieking touch-line; THEY don't know what it is like to move in an 'aesthetic' set. THEY don't know what it is to be a slave and to have one, to be booted round like a lump of dirt and afterwards do the same to other people; yes, there is manliness in us all, but wait till we meet a crisis; wait till we come across a game that is played with *guts*, ah, sweet word; then perhaps old fumbling, slobbering, unpractical R.C.H. may have a chance, who knows...

It is difficult not to hear the sounds of war lying behind the evocations of 'crisis'. R.C.H. was 7 when the First World War was declared and 12 when it ended and the impact of war on those who fought and, in particular, the surviving families, was to be a central issue in many of his novels. He shows little enthusiasm for his compulsory activities in the school Cadet Corps. The prospect of 1939 seems all too real in his imagination in 1923.

The immediate crisis, however was what lay ahead after Monkton and this was solved by his family and school encouraging him to apply to Oxford (though he had thought of trying to follow in Sheldon's footsteps in Cambridge) and he successfully obtained a place at Oriel College.

His final ambiguous feelings about leaving school and entering the 'real' world are starkly summarised in a dramatic, rhetorical declaration: 'Farewell red book, hold well your secret, and, tomorrow: farewell Monkton, you joyous, miserable hole; farewell all!'

R.C.H.'s parents and sister: (left to right) Mabel, Madge, R.C.H., Harry.

R.C.H. aged 17.

Opening page of R.C.H.'s Schoolboy diary. His "red book."

Opening page of R.C.H.'s first novel, *The Hand of the Purple Idol.* His habit of constant revision is evident in the first line.

MONKTON COMBE SCHOOL, 1st XV., 1923.

A. F. Kitching, Esq., R. C. Hutchinson, G. H. P. Gibbs, T. R. H. Chalcraft, H. Brown, C. W. W. Elwell, J. C. Walkey, W. I. Madge-Forman, Rev. E. S. Hunt
(Coach)   (Coach)
K. D. A. Howard, M. W. Gonin, R. H. W. Pakenham, R. S. L. Chappell, J. E. S. Fox
(Vice-Capt.)   (Capt.)
J. H. W. James   C. N. Royal   J. M. Greenwood

R.C.H. standing, second right. Of the 17 pictured 5 were to become ordained or become missionaries, and 3 were first class athletes. Muscular Christianity was alive and well at Monkton in the 1920s.

Chapter 2

Oxford, Norwich, and the First Novel

Oriel College, the fifth-oldest Oxford college, founded in 1326, lies in the heart of the city. It is not clear why it was chosen as a suitable college for R.C.H. (its prowess on the river may have been one appealing factor), but the college had other historic traditions which reflected his intellectual interests. He could have chosen to study English Literature – a very new academic discipline – but perhaps he felt that as a constant reader, and seeing literature as a 'hobby', he wished to explore his growing interests in political theories and religious and philosophical ideas, and the new course of PPE (Politics, Philosophy, and Economics), only established in 1920, seemed an attractive alternative. Oriel has been described as 'the acknowledged centre of Oxford intellectualism' in the nineteenth century and was certainly at the heart of the theological and ecclesiastical controversies surrounding the 'Oxford Movement'. It was the college which could count among its fellows, John Henry Newman, John Keble, Edward Bouverie Pusey, and Matthew Arnold. J.A. Froude was also an undergraduate. R.C.H. could hardly not have been intrigued by the character of Newman who, at the age of 15 (the same age that R.C.H. was writing his diary), converted to evangelical Christianity, the truth of which he was 'more certain of than I have hands and feet'. Becoming a Calvinist, Newman was convinced that the Pope was the Antichrist. He could have come straight from the Coryton family. By the age of 44, Newman had converted to Roman Catholicism, becoming a Cardinal in 1879, and was canonised in 2019.

R.C.H. made some life-long friends. One was A.J.P. Taylor, later to become a distinguished and popular historian of left-wing views. Intriguingly their friendship sprang not from intellectual discussions in college rooms but from being fellow members of a college rowing crew. Another friendship was formed with Harold Hobson, who was to make his name as a influential theatre critic, and with J.I.M. Stewart, an acknowledged expert on the writings of Joseph Conrad – a writer often seen, together with Dickens and Balzac, as a major influence on R.C.H. (Stewart was also a popular crime writer under the pseudonym Michael Innes – a transposition of his two middle Christian names). Charles Wrinch, later a charismatic teacher of English at Radley College (and briefly headmaster of Raynes Park County School) was another close friend.

R.C.H. keenly pursued his rowing enthusiasm but developed a new and absorbing interest in flying. He joined the cavalry section of the Officers' Training Corps but found that he had no natural rapport with horses, so switched his allegiance and became a founder member of the University Air Squadron. Fifty years later, R.C.H. recalled with amusement in a letter to his friend Martyn Skinner his first encounter with riding a horse.

> Incidentally, if the horse is the friend of man it proved a poor friend to me... At Oxford, I thought I would learn to manage one of those beasts, at the taxpayers' expense, by joining the cavalry section of the O.U.O.T.C. For my first recruits' parade I borrowed breeches from an enormous man called Le Mesurier ... not realising that he had exceptionally narrow calves and thighs. When I had got this garment on, my legs would not bend at all. Somehow I arrived at the riding school, where the other recruits were going round and round in a long file with great dignity and confidence, and an enormous nag was brought to me. 'Mount!' said the riding sergeant. I did not see how this was to be done – the port-side pedal on this brute was roughly level with my chin. Some grooms took pity on me and heaved me aboard, and I was ordered to join the back of the circulating file. But how? I made clucking noises, the horse turned his head to look at me with infinite boredom. Again the grooms were charitable – one of them gave the beast what Dickens calls a shrewd cuff, on the starboard

buttock; he (the horse) responded by setting off at full gallop and joining *the front* of the file with the sergeant shouting 'Watcherthinkyerupto, Mistruchinkson – riding in the Derby?' It was all gravely embarrassing. How thankful I was after a year of such humiliations, to transfer to the Air Squadron. Many things may be argued against the aeroplane, but if treated with reasonable consideration it does *not* turn round and rush back to barracks entirely of its own accord, or plunge under trees with low boughs which admit its passage but not the passage of its pilot.

His constant claim in his 'red book' that he was unpractical was true enough – domestically his expertise went little beyond washing-up and lightbulb changing, but he was fascinated by movement and travel (though rarely travelling himself). He may not have known what happened under the bonnet of a car, but he loved driving, and counted it one of life's paternal pleasures to teach his children to drive. ('I love going in a car at ninety miles an hour – so long as I am driving and so long as it is not my car.') Travel, by any means – train, car, boat, aeroplane – is a constant motif in his novels: it enables journeys towards a search for some self-knowledge; the varying speed of travel mirroring the progression of such discoveries, either positive or otherwise, and the pivotal moments are often at quay-sides, in train carriages, and ultimately at railway stations. Perhaps when flying an aeroplane he felt himself in a similar role as he was playing as a novelist – in control of a powerful creation, but always aware that he was only a partial controller of other influences more powerful than his own.

His decision to read PPE. had far more reaching significance than just an academic one. He had become strongly attracted, at lectures, to a fellow PPE undergraduate from Lady Margaret Hall. He claimed that it had almost been 'love at first sight' when he caught sight of her in the foyer of the Examination Schools and said to himself: 'If I ever have any children, that's the girl I want them to call "Mummy".' Their relationship began in a rather bizarre way, involving (perhaps appropriately, considering R.C.H.'s fascination with travel and vehicles) bicycles. His natural shyness prevented him from any direct personal introduction, but at lectures he left anonymous notes in the basket of her bicycle and hearing that she had been reprimanded for riding her bicycle without a rear light, he secretly deposited a cycle lamp, with a note, in her college pigeon hole. After some careful investigation (she thought she recognised the handwriting from the note-taking of a fellow student) she discovered who the knight in disguise must be, and a relationship began. Her name was Margaret Owen Jones, daughter of Captain Owen Jones CBE (of the Merchant Navy). By the archaic rules of the university in the 1920s, no junior members were allowed to entertain members of the opposite sex in college premises unless accompanied by a chaperone approved by the proctors (the university 'police'). In February 1927 R.C.H. wrote his first hesitant note to Margaret (though touched with some facetiousness):

> Dear Miss Owen Jones,
>
> I trust you will overlook the very great liberty I am taking in writing to you. An even more reprehensible breach of etiquette is to follow:
>
> I wonder if you could consider me sufficiently introduced to ask if you would care to have tea with me in my rooms some day next week? If you can forgive my audacity, I should be very delighted to entertain you, with 'a companion similarly approved' ('*Vide:* Memorandum on the Conduct and Discipline of Junior Members of the University, P.4) at the address above at about 4 o'clock on Monday, Tuesday or Wednesday next. Should you feel it proper to ignore this invitation entirely I shall fully understand your position.
>
> > With renewed apologies,
> > Believe me,
> > Yours sincerely,
> > R.Coryton Hutchinson.

She replied on the same day:

> Dear Mr. Hutchinson,
>
> I think, although I have only known who you are for two days, I have evidence of your kindness in my possession enough to serve as ample introduction! I therefore have much pleasure in accepting your kind invitation for Monday at 4 o'clock, and will bring with me a companion whom I think you, as well as the Proctors, will 'similarly approve.'
>
> > Yours sincerely,
> > Margaret Owen Jones.

It became something of a whirlwind romance. There were many more meetings over tea, and excursions to local Cotswold villages. Margaret was a loyal spectator at R.C.H's rowing races, but she was also a keen sportswoman herself. She had played hockey and tennis at her school in Guildford and was a more than respectable field athlete – catching the eye of the sports reporter from the *Oxford Gazette* when she achieved second place in the long-jump at a Lady Margaret Hall sports event. After that nervous invitation to tea in February 1927 many long letters passed between them, which developed in terms of address from the formality of 'Miss Owen Jones' and 'R.Coryton Hutchinson' through 'Ray Dear' and 'Darling' to 'My own beloved man', 'Darling girl', and 'Your loving, loving Margaret'. Within six months they had become engaged.

They shared some anxieties about how their future parents-in-law would react to their relationship and how the two families would react to each other. Captain Owen Jones firmly represented a tradition that revered 'manliness' and discipline: Margaret described him as 'viewing the present generation as absolutely decadent and seeing no good in anyone under forty'. On the Hutchinson side, R.C.H. had always been uncomfortable with the snobbery of the Coryton side of the family, complaining in the 'red book' that his parents' engagement was first broken off because his mother's family 'objected to a match with one who could not trace his [Family] tree through more than three generations'. He wrote to Margaret: 'It is a hereditary failing of the Coryton family that they are either snobs or religious fanatics, some of them both, but they are all very charming in other respects.' He recorded an amusing slant to this aspect of Coryton characteristics:

> We had an old friend of Muzzie's staying with us. She is a charming person, very generous, but I have seldom met anyone with such violent prejudices (nationalistic, diehard etc.) and she has the snobbery of two Corytons rolled into one. She talks at length of D.G. Rossetti, to whom she is related, and her next-door neighbour Max Beerbohm. Max, as a matter of fact, seems well worth talking about.

But their misgivings quickly proved to be unfounded. Perhaps the Owen Jones family were more relaxed about having a literary-minded son-in-law because of his manly pursuits of rowing and flying. Within a few weeks Margaret was describing conversations at home with her father describing R.C.H. as 'such a sensible, dependable fellow', and her mother referring to him as 'a dear boy'. Similarly, R.C.H. frequently assured her that 'My family adores you.'

There was, however, one dark cloud which hovered over these pleasant future hopes. Margaret's brother, Patrick, had become a schoolmaster immediately after leaving university. He was of a nervous disposition and lacked self-confidence. After two terms of teaching he travelled to Scotland. One morning his clothes were found neatly folded on the banks of the icy cold water of a loch. His body was never discovered. The verdict was an 'open' one. It seemed unbelievable to both Margaret and R.C.H. that Patrick would have chosen to leap into the freezing water and be drowned in an inexplicable accident. Margaret felt strongly that she had not sufficiently defended her brother from his feelings of having failed to rise to the manly expectations of his family. (Was his swimming an act of defiance or an attempt at proving his masculinity?). The event also awakened some guilty feelings in R.C.H. about how he had sometimes treated his sister, Madge. He had confessed to his diary that 'I am inclined to be harsh with her.' In a later novel he was to create a narrator who observes of one character: 'Her jejune greeting had pleased me; it was of the sisterly shape, and sisters are of a class too little valued.' Certainly he was to become, as a novelist, sensitive to 'outsiders' within family units. In fact, Madge was to follow in this sympathetic direction, joining the probation service and becoming a probation inspector and tutor at the Home Office. R.C.H. was to include a drowning, which may have been an accident or suicide, in his novel *Shining Scabbard.*

Meanwhile there were academic obligations to face – in R.C.H.'s case the challenge of 'finals'. He complained that the exam questions concentrated almost entirely on topics about which he was least confident. He was summoned to a *viva* exam (the university's oral interviews, usually intended to decide which class of degree should be awarded to candidates who were 'on the edge'). R.C.H. realised that he was on the border between a second- and third-class degree and was bitterly disappointed to find himself awarded a third. He received an encouraging letter from his tutor E.L. Hargreaves who told him that he 'remained on the line till the end and only just missed your second'. Perhaps he found some comfort from his 'moral tutor',

Marcus Todd, who assured him that throughout his Oriel career 'you have given me no moments of misgiving or anxiety'.

To divert his disappointment he threw himself with enthusiasm into a flying course at Manston on the Kent coast and achieved his long-held ambition to fly solo, much enjoying the exhilaration of seeing the Kent countryside rolling beneath him.

The next problem was to find employment, at least for the next year until Margaret had taken her finals and they could get married. He was still determined to make writing his ultimate goal but was realistic enough to see that marriage and domestic life made some reliable income necessary. He was fortunate to have some family influences to draw on – an uncle of R.C.H.'s, who had been superintendent of the vice-regal estates in India, arranged an introduction which resulted in an offer of a commercial job in Bombay, and Margaret had Indian cousins. Margaret's father had contacts at the Bank of England and with the Duchy of Lancaster, both of which made offers of possible employment, and Charles Wrinch's family had connections in East Anglia, which was where a final opening emerged: an appointment, somewhat surprisingly, as assistant advertising manager for Colman's mustard, at £250 a year. This was mostly a matter of desk work, but also involved some requirement to visit restaurants and hotels to encourage businesses to use his firm's products – a duty which conflicted sharply with his natural shyness. So in late 1927 R.C.H. found himself living in a bedsit in Norwich, a daily office worker, waiting for Margaret (who had confidently achieved a second-class degree) to join him after their wedding in April 1929, when they moved to larger accommodation in the city.

Colman's had an intriguing history of literary connections in the 1920s. In 1922, Dorothy Sayers joined the advertising agency of S.H. Benson and worked on the portfolio for Colman's mustard (presumably the basis for her detective novel *Murder must Advertise*) and created the highly successful 'Mustard Club' which featured in advertisements on London buses, were common in cartoons, had its own newsletter and badges, published its own recipe book, and the music hall star Harry Far released a 78-rpm single record featuring the club. Sayers left Benson's in 1931 and there is no evidence that R.C.H. ever met her when he joined Colman's, but he must have been aware of her prominent position within Colman's publicity department.

But neither mustard nor marriage could keep him away from his pen and his desk. As a relief from the tedium of hours spent over ledgers at Colman's office (rather evocative of a Dickensian scene) he spent almost every spare hour planning literary schemes. In January 1928 he had his first breakthrough when a short story, 'Every Twenty Years' (started in his last few months at Oxford) was published in *Empire Review*. But his mind was working on a grander scale and within nine months he was at work on his first full-scale novel, *Thou Hast A Devil*.

Twenty years later, looking back over his writing career, he dismissed the novel, with typical modesty and forthrightness, as 'a wad of balderdash'. Writing for *The Listener* he recalled:

> Not long ago, I was poking about in a secondhand bookshop in Lincoln, and I was suddenly confronted by a copy of a novel with the awkward title *Thou Hast A Devil*. It was my first published book. The cover was mildewed, but it had not suffered from any hard usage, so I bought it – it cost me 4d. – meaning to put it in the first convenient stove. On the way home, in the train, I opened it and read a few paragraphs. And I said to myself: '*Is this excruciating work a faithful portrait of my own mind when I was twenty-one?*'
>
> When I tried to get back inside that adolescent mind – to think and feel exactly as I had thought and felt twenty-five years before – I found that it could not be done. I remembered, of course, the circumstances in which the book was written. They were not romantic. I was not starving in a garret, and I did not write on the backs of menus or race-cards. I was living by myself in a flat – or what counted for a flat – in the city of Norwich in 1929, and during the day I was employed by a firm of manufacturers in covering large sheets of paper with very tiny figures – for what purpose I never exactly discovered. This was an especially cold winter; and on days when there was thick snow on the ground, the old lady who was supposed to come in and 'do' for me did not arrive; so I used to get home in the evenings to find my bed unmade and my greasy breakfast things still on the table. Before that situation could be dealt with, the waste pipe of the sink had to be unfrozen with kettles of boiling water. It was only when all this sordid housewifery had been disposed of – that is to say, about eight or nine o'clock – that I could get down to

my 'masterpiece', and I wrote something like 1,000 words
a night… But then, in most ways, one's first book is much
the easiest to write… You are quite un-self-critical. Any
joke you manufacture seems to you vastly amusing, your
dialogue sounds commendably similar to the dialogue you
have read in other people's books, your descriptive passages
appear to you shrewdly turned and rather harmonious…
All I wanted was to produce a *book*… No, wait! It is not
true to say I *only* hoped to produce a book. What I wanted,
and I am confessing to a degree of fatuity which now appals
me, was to turn out a 'brilliant' book.

The novel certainly has an intriguing setting and theme: a
rendering of the New Testament story in an imaginary near future
time when people travelled by enormous luxury airships (R.C.H.'s
most exotic choice of various means of transport). The whole
book might be seen as a dramatic portrayal of the 'red book',
for all the major elements appear in a kind of three-dimensional
autobiography seen through the eyes of the hero, Guy, who is seen
leaving Oxford to take up a commercial job (arranged through
family connections) selling meat-extract and fish-paste (instead of
mustard) in a distant part of the British Empire, Strainland. Guy
has possibly studied at Oriel – he has certainly been influenced by
Matthew Arnold:

> Guy had never admitted it to anyone, but in his schooldays
> he had always thought that Cambridge was the better place –
> until he had chanced to read the 'Essays in Criticism', and
> had inevitably fallen under the spell of Oxford's greatest
> publicist. Well, here were 'the last enchantments of the
> Middle Age'. Arnold, unlike most advertisers, had been
> perfectly honest – if anything too restrained. 'Beauty, which
> is only Truth seen from another side'. And here was beauty,
> not sensuous and intoxicating, but cool, majestic, persuasive;
> Beauty, calmly asserting that it was the beginning and end of
> all reason, the only perfection which could never weary by its
> perfectness. *This* was Oxford. The thousands of young men
> who spent a mad three years there, reading easily-forgotten
> books and rowing monotonously up and down the river …

only a few of them caught the reflection of beauty and shone it into the world.

R.C.H.'s memory of seeing the crippled beggar in Haymarket is recreated when Guy, as an undergraduate, is rebuked by his companion when he gives money to a crippled beggar: 'You shouldn't encourage those bounders. That fellow was obviously a humbug. I don't mind betting his left arm was as good as his right. All charity is irrational.' Guy responded: 'I'm equally prepared to bet he needed half-a-crown more than I do.' There is plenty of opportunity for Guy to put his social and political conscience to the test for Strainland is in the middle of social and commercial upheaval: the workers are being exploited by their white bosses while Guy is supposed 'to sell beef-extract to starving natives living on a handful of rice a day'; Guy is appalled by the accepted racism in the paternal, patronising attitude of the white 'rulers': 'the Strains are quite good chappies but you've got to keep 'em in their place'. (Less generous white settlers refer not to 'chappies' but to 'ruddy niggers'.)

But there is an even stronger thematic strain running through the novel which is inherently intertwined with the economic and political issues: religion. All the problems and controversies covered in R.C.H.'s Monkton diary make their appearances in Strainland. Everything centres on the figure of a charismatic faith healer, Khamhaiv. Distrusted by the white community who see him as a political activist, though he is at heart a pacifist, he has a magnetic pull on Guy. The white community see even his religious convictions as a threat to social peace: 'Khamhaiv's one of these preachin' and teachin' natives – sort of tries to cut the missionaries out … Mystics make the natives uppish, you know.' R.C.H. must have had some knowledge, through his family association with India and through Margaret's Indian connections, with the political upheavals in India over self-rule; from time to time, missionaries had been discouraged from going to British India. Guy has been deeply impressed by a conversation with one of Strainland's Mandus (priests) who sees the connection of religion and economics as part of the West's attempts to destroy native culture:

'You think, then, that it would have been better if the English had never come to Strainland at all?'
   'I certainly do!' replied the Mandu…

'But', Guy continued... 'don't you think that the removal of British control would at once plunge the whole country, with its hundred and one sects and races, into a turmoil of civil discord?'

'The British', the priest replied, 'are very useful as a police force...Under the pretence of keeping order they make laws to suit their ends, they enrich themselves vastly, and they proclaim to the whole world their virtue and altruism in looking after us poor natives; they make no effort to understand our national character or our aspirations. As the great Roman Imperialist expressed it, they make a desert, and they call it peace.'

All this echoed what Guy had expressed when musing on a train journey (a typical place for such enlightenment) earlier in the novel:

He had made it his practice from time to time to see, as far as he could, how the other half of the world lived. He had come to the conclusion that the reason why rich people annoyed him was their ignorance rather than their callousness ... he continually encountered men and women in clubs and drawing-rooms who, so far from caring how less fortunate members of society lived, didn't even know ... He was forever hearing the overfed and over-dressed say, 'There aren't any poor people nowadays. What with these pensions and doles and one thing and another ... the working-classes are as idle and well-off as anyone. I heard of a chimney-sweep the other day who sent his son to Eton. *I* had to sell my Daimler to do that.'

The character of Khamhaiv was the key figure to unify all these questions and tensions in Guy's mind. He saw him as both a faith healer and a healer of faith who will bring personal freedom rather than revolutionary political freedom. It is easy to see the lack of subtlety in the Christian allegorical characterisation of Khamhaiv: he is a motor mechanic rather than a carpenter; he begins to speak in Christ-like vocabulary: 'I must fall at their hands, and no one must try to save me. But my message must remain, and thrive, and spread ... I am stronger than men.' He proves to be a good Samaritan by saving a girl in distress and insisting on rescuing her attacker and ensuring that he is taken care of; after Khamhaiv's arrest as a political agitator he is passed from one authority to another before being condemned to death after his accuser has received a kiss. Finally, after his supposed death, he is seen by a small group of his followers (including Guy and his friend Shadowford) in 'an upper room'. As Khamhaiv leaves, he is given a glass of water poured from Guy's hipflask and leaves it on a window ledge. When Shadowford takes a sip, he declares in 'a shout that was whispered: It isn't water. It's wine.'

But the novel is not just a social, political, and theological essay, it is full of varied tones. It can be very funny, especially in the portrayal of the speech and actions of upper-class members of the Damocles club in Oxford, the Eton and Sandhurst educated Major Dane and the shooting, hunting, and womanising John Brushing. There is a tender romantic relationship between Guy and the Governor's daughter, Diana. There are some memorable character portraits. After witnessing an assassination attempt, he describes the Governor's wife's reaction:

> As far as she took any interest in her own personality Theodora believed that this incident, *the* incident of her life, had killed her soul; but in reality her soul was not dead – all the branches had been lopped off and the vitality which was thus denied egress had been forced into one splendid green shoot, so well hidden beneath the stump of a bough that no one noticed it.

The problem of finding a publisher was solved by a piece of good fortune. Margaret's mother was a friend of the popular right-wing journalist and prolific novelist, Sir Philip Gibbs. He was sufficiently impressed by the manuscript to introduce R.C.H. to his agent, and it was published by Ernest Benn in October 1930, the only time R.C.H. published under the name Ray Coryton Hutchinson. His next ten novels were to be published by Cassells, before Geoffrey Bles took over for three novels and Michael Joseph for the final three. R.C.H. recalled: 'It was thanks to the kindness of Philip Gibbs who gave me a personal introduction to his literary agent, that this preposterous work did, after many days and many journeys, get published. It earned me £27.' It went into a second edition five years later, with very limited circulation, and has been, for the next 85 years, a rare volume.

It received four reviews, two from provincial papers in Nottingham, one from the *Morning Post,* and a brief one in *The Times Literary Supplement.* Inevitably they sound rather like end-of-term reports, suggesting promise for the future: 'Mr. Hutchinson has ideas and imagination and should do good work in the future.' 'Mr. Hutchinson possesses such a vivid imagination.' 'Its original theme and genuine, sturdy thoughts make it an outstanding publication.'

He had, however, achieved his first step on his ambition to be a writer and could celebrate the publication of seeing a novel in print. Guy, of course, is a fictional character and not a portrait of R.C.H. But as a portrayal of a young man exploring the challenges of adulthood it has much to commend it, in particular its suggestion of where answers might lie without any dogmatic declaration that the characters have found some easy answers. Guy describes himself succinctly. He was:

> turning over in his mind the doubts and questions with which school has left him ... two years in an unusually brilliant sixth form, much of that time spent in public and private debating had stripped the certainty from all his childish convictions. He had felt that, from religion to chemistry, nothing, however obvious it seemed, could be regarded as dogmatic truth.

Guy found no greater certainty from his university career for:

> troubled by this agnosticism, as boys in the growing period are troubled, he had thought that Oxford, with its mysterious, paternal solemnity, the home of sound learning and true religion, would give him back something wherein to put his faith. But Oxford had given him no creed other than the reinforcement of his doubts, no prophet but an elderly don who had told him in a musical tone that the most important thing to know is that we know nothing. Guy smiled at the reflection.

The reader is left with a haunting image from a conversation when Guy unexpectedly meets Khamhaiv and asks him: 'Is idealism reconcilable with practical politics? Can a man enjoy the view and tie up his shoes at the same time?' Khamhaiv replies: 'Yes – raise one foot at a time, so they form part of the view.' *Thou Hast A Devil* may show some of the signs of a 'first attempt' at novel writing, but one thing that it isn't is 'a wad of balderdash'.

R.C.H.'s closest Oxford Friends.

Harold Hobson.

J.I.M. Stewart (Michael Innes), on the cover of his autobiography.

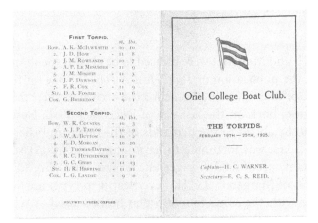

Oriel Second Torpid. R.C.H. at 6, A.J.P Taylor at 2.

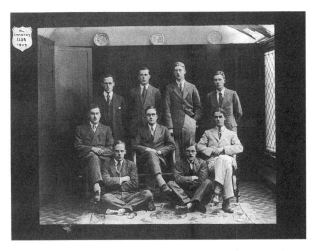

Oriel Chantry Club 1927. R.C.H. seated left, second row;
Charles Wrinch seated right, second row.

Chapter 3

Four Early Novels

R.C.H. and Margaret were pleased to be able to spend the £27 earned from the publication of *Thou Hast A Devil* to pay for the services of a doctor and a nursing home for the arrival of their first child, Ann Coryton, born on the last day of December 1930. Now parenthood was to be added to the demands of the office and the writing desk, but R.C.H. was fortunate to have found an enthusiastic secretarial assistant, proof-reader, eager encourager, and shrewd critic in the person of Margaret. R.C.H. never learnt to type, nor wanted to. He wrote with the same fountain pen he had used at school, dipping the nib into the ink bottle. Until sufficient funds had allowed for the employment of professional help, Margaret typed the first two novels and, in the case of *Thou Hast A Devil*, R.C.H. 'lovingly dedicates this fable to the typist, who despite what she suffered in transcribing the author's manuscript, was yet so rash as to marry the author'. He always described Margaret as 'my chief literary adviser' and she wrote to him early in his move to Norwich: 'you must go on writing when you have time and ideas, and we'll see you famous yet. I don't think you're the sort of man to let business take away your imagination. I do hope we both keep our imagination all through our life.' Their relationship was as rich a creative partnership as a personal one.

One of the characteristics of R.C.H.'s style is that every novel is *sui generis*, in tone and often in form. This may be one explanation for his uneven popularity in terms of readership. He followed no trend, paid no allegiance to anything beyond his own artistic convictions: 'I have always written exactly what and how I wanted ... if you do that you can't expect a very large audience. I have never made allowances for my reader.' This element of his creative stance is linked to an imagination which, like his obsession with travel, was always on the move. No sooner had he written the final sentence of one novel than he was working on the next, sometimes having two in his mind simultaneously. Within a few weeks of completing *Thou Hast A Devil* he was composing a quite different script: a novel, comic in tone, consisting of letters from a young man to his maiden aunt, entitled *The Caravan Of Culture*. He seemed only half confident of its quality (his self-confessed youthful 'un-self-critical' approach to his work was quickly being refined), and this was evident in his intention to publish under a pseudonym, Patricia Post. He described it as a 'trivial pot-boiler' and it certainly failed to boil any pots as it was the only completed adult novel to remain unpublished.

There is no evidence that he ever had any contact with Graham Greene, or had read any of his novels, but they certainly shared many interesting characteristics, which were evident even from this early period. Separated in age by less than three years, and briefly overlapping as Oxford undergraduates, they both wrote about religious doubts and challenges, even if from different theological perspectives – Greene often seen as the doyen of twentieth-century Catholic novelists. R.C.H. would certainly have sympathy with Greene's aversion to being described as a 'Roman Catholic' writer rather than as a novelist who happened to be a Catholic. Greene also often combined serious themes with the elements of the thriller. R.C.H. shared this attractive juxtaposition, evident in some of his own novels such as *March the Ninth*. Forty years after R.C.H.'s unsuccessful pot-boiler about a young man's relationship with his maiden aunt, Greene published his highly successful pot-boiler about a nephew's relationship with his (supposed) maiden aunt in his novel *Travels With My Aunt*.

After setting aside *The Caravan Of Culture*, R.C.H. was much happier with what was in his mind, and was to emerge as his second published novel, *The Answering Glory*. The reader's immediate response might easily be that here was a novel completely different from *Thou Hast A Devil*. We are not taken to a strange land, at an undefined time, by means of flamboyant transport; we are placed firmly in the 1930s, partly in southern England and partly in an imaginary remote and sparsely populated island off the coast of Africa. We are asked to see events not through the eyes of an idealistic young man, but from the perspective of two very different females – an elderly spinster and a young school-leaver. We are not asked to reflect on social, economic, and political philosophies, with some passing witty observations on social pretensions described through external physical cameos of behaviour and modes of speech and conversation. R.C.H. has moved to more internal observations of characters' hopes and convictions, however eccentric, and although the tone is mostly humorous, it is laughter more often derived from sympathetic understanding than from external caricature. It is probably the novel which exhibits R.C.H.'s control of pathos more acutely than any other.

The novel's central issue remains, however, as in the first novel: religion. But the focus this time is on how characters react to their individual experiences and suggests no particular preferred route to enlightenment. If *Thou Hast A Devil* sees life through the lens of an imaginary telescope, R.C.H. has changed his artistic optical aid to a magnifying glass, now being viewed through more mature and objective eyes.

The central character is an elderly Plymouth Brethren missionary, Miss Thompson (her first name is never revealed), who has spent her life dedicated to converting the inhabitants of the unhealthy swamps of São Maharo. She has taught herself enough basic medicine to provide the only medical facility available, and her home doubles as a daily surgery, her patients seeing her as the bringer of all goodness and wisdom, devoted to her as the accepted matriarch and arbiter of disputes among this impoverished and disease-ridden island. Her few free hours are spent on turning the Talusa tongue – they have no written form of language – into an orally memorable version of the gospels. She may be frail in stature but she is fearless and invincible in spirit. Undaunted by physical or natural dangers she travels by canoe through crocodile-infested waters to restrain a powerful, drunken native attempting to kill his wife for giving birth to a still-born son. She confronts the 15-stone raving figure, orders him to be tied and bound until he sobers up. She forms a particularly strong bond with a young boy, Peter, who appoints himself as a personal servant to 'Mother Thompson' and reports for duty on a daily basis.

Miss Thompson only feels at home in Maharo and is determined to be buried on Maharan soil. Unfortunately she succumbs to the violent hossi fever of the Talusas and is forced to return to England for treatment and recuperation. She promises: 'I SHALL COME BACK.'

Every day Peter makes the arduous journey across the forest and climbs the steep rock-face to have a view of the sea to watch out for the sign of a ship bringing back 'Mother Thompson'. Every day, for several months, he returns through the dark trees, sad and frightened: 'She does not come', he cries.

Once in England, the tone changes. Miss Thompson may not bat an eyelid travelling by canoe to pacify a drunken, murderous Talusan, but is quite unable to make a journey through London, involving buses and the underground, without a chaperone. Always terrified as to whether she is complying with etiquette or not, even a visit to a tea shop is an expedition involving fear of social solecisms. Such excursions are interspersed with evocative descriptions of meetings with the tireless Miss Green, surrounded by bulging files and piles of letters in the cobwebbed office of Miss Warrener's Womens' Missionary Society.

Miss Thompson is sent for convalescence to Mrs Fuller's boarding house for missionaries on furlough. There are delightful descriptions of life in such establishments, including breakfasts:

> The brown dish-cover had not yet been lifted, but they knew it was dried haddock. Still, it would be boiled eggs tomorrow – haddock had not yet been so impertinent as to appear on a Sunday – and there was a good chance that they would not be under-boiled, as a very tactful remark had been made last Sunday about under-boiling; they might be hard-boiled, but you could always put in a little piece of butter if Mrs. Fuller's attention was engaged. Tomorrow was also the day for a clean cloth and clean napkins ; it would be the blue check, the two yellow check having run their course. The blue check was brighter and jollier than the yellow ones. The present cloth had reached a very dingy stage (Mrs. Fuller saw no point in removing it between meals; there was a little desk for the ladies to do their writing and sewing could be done on the sofa)... Miss Thompson watched the plates. She was hoping to get the one with the three chips in the edge. That one, she knew, was alright. There was one with a crack right across, and a little tributary crack forming a narrow segment. It was bound to break before long...

It is a world as vivid as that to be captured 20 years later by Barbara Pym. Miss Thompson is treated by the kindly Dr Crewe who observes to himself that all the missionaries under his care seem to have something in common: 'restlessness, a kind of beautiful insanity'. This 'insanity' comes to the fore in the middle section of the novel, set in the exclusive, evangelical girls' boarding school, Huntersfield, dedicated to hockey and Christianity, under the watchful eye of the Principal, The Honourable Augusta Lesage. It reads like a parody of the novels of Angela Brazil – at her most popular at the time of the writing of *The Answering Glory*. Huntersfield is to provide the audience for the distressed Miss Thompson who has rashly volunteered, at 24 hours' notice, to give a lecture replacing an indisposed missionary. All she has is a set of slides depicting an African country which she has never visited and a set of notes she cannot decipher. But before she faces this ordeal she is subjected to a guided tour of the school's new laboratory by the senior science mistress, Miss Halliwell. Miss Thompson knows nothing about Physics or Chemistry and is fearful of not showing sufficient interest or, worse still, of asking embarrassing questions:

> Miss Thompson gazed at a row of jars. If only there was one labelled H_2SO_4 she would be able to show that she was not without education. Miss Halliwell moved towards her first exhibit.
> 'This is the G. and M. Universal Spectrophotometer.'
> 'Oh, yes.'
> 'These are chainomatic balances.'
> 'Oh, I see,'
> Miss Thompson gazed at the chainomatic balances. Miss Halliwell courteously gave her full time to absorb their features, before moving on.
> 'This is another chainomatic balance,' she said.
> 'Oh, you have several?'
> 'Yes, three.'...
> 'This,' said Miss Halliwell gloomily, 'is the Van Slyke manometric gas apparatus. It's rather an up-to-date type – the Bale-Stoney.'
> 'What does it do?'
> 'Oh, we use it chiefly for the microanalysis of blood.'
> 'Oh, I see.'...
> 'I expect you've seen a Rehwald micro-burette?'

'No, I don't think so.'

'Oh. This is one.'

'Oh, yes.'

We're rather proud of this,' Miss Halliwell said without enthusiasm, 'not many schools have them.'

'What is it?'

'It's a Lovibond Tintometer.'

'Oh, yes.'

'Would you like to see the new lecture-room?'

'I would, very much.'

Miss Haliwell led the way up a few stairs, opened another door, and stood aside for Miss Thompson to see in...

'Oh, is this the lecture room?' Miss Halliwell admitted that it was the lecture-room...

'Is there anything more?' Miss Thompson wondered. 'I must show appreciation somehow, it's so good of her to take all this trouble. Oh, we've got back to the same room, so we must have seen everything.' 'This is the senior physics lab.,' Miss Halliwell said remorselessly. (Oh, then it wasn't the same room! But it looked exactly the same.) 'This is a thermohydrograph.'

Miss Thompson examined the thermohydrograph carefully.

'It's rather like the – the thing we saw in the other room,' she suggested.

'Oh, do you think so?' Miss Halliwell asked with cold politeness.

'Well, just a little bit.'

'Oh.' Miss Halliwell moved on. 'This is rather interesting – an autographic Atwood machine.'

'Yes, very interesting... Do you find teaching interesting?'

'No, not very.'

'That's a pity.'

'Yes.'

There can have been few less relaxing moments before Miss Thompson found herself on the platform, stumbling through her lecture. In an attempt to rescue some dignity she returned to familiar territory and for the last few minutes spoke of her own experiences and work in São Maharo. Little could she guess how influential those

last words were to be on the life of one girl in the audience, Barbara –
in her last few weeks at school, and who had little, if any, religious
enthusiasms.

The girls at Huntersfield divided themselves into two groups –
the 'piety squad' who attended prayer meetings, and a more cynical
squad who saw little point in the values which the school attempted
to instil. It was from this latter group that Barbara emerged. She
despised anyone who didn't display defiance or show – her favourite
word – 'guts'. (One recalls R.C.H.'s phrase in the 'red book': *'guts,*
ah, sweet word'). Barbara turns on a giggling group of girls who are
making fun of Miss Thompson's fumbling lecture: 'My God! If you
little swine had got a tenth of that woman's guts you'd be of some
use in the world.' And so, within months, this worldly, cigarette-
smoking, whisky-drinking young lady, with flimsy obvious religious
piety, follows in the footsteps of Miss Thompson (whose final semi-
conscious conviction is that she has returned to São Mahara) and
journeys to attempt to replace Miss Thompson among the Talusas.
R.C.H. often had several possible titles for a novel, and one in an early
draft for *The Answering Glory* is tellingly, *Strange Return*.

The *actual* title is taken from a line in a poem by Robert Louis
Stevenson, 'If This Were Faith', which extols bravery in the face of
suffering, both at 'Golgotha and Khartoum'. R.C.H. later wrote:

> You might perhaps say that the book is a *story,* and not some
> form of propaganda dressed up as a story; and that the theme
> of the book is courage as humanity's highest common
> denomination (to use a clumsy expression). The suggestion
> being that courage takes its place besides Love as part of
> the main strength of Christianity.

A pivotal moment for Barbara as she struggles to decide why she
wishes to go San Marino comes on a visit to the studio of her artist
father. This is to become a familiar setting for critical moments in
the novels, and paintings – particularly portraits – often form the
focus of such scenes. In *The Stepmother* a portrait almost takes on
the role of a character within the novel. In Barbara's case, Dr Crewe's
observation of the 'beautiful insanity' of his patients is combined
with Barbara's father's thoughts on the world of the artist. He has
asked whether Barbara's desire to follow Miss Thompson is purely 'an
adventure'. She replies:

'No. There's nothing so stupid as an objectless adventure. It's an adventure to jump off the top of a bus, but it's not worth doing'…

'You know, I'm afraid you're a Quixote.'

'Well, aren't you? You're only really happy when you're painting something only a dozen or so people can appreciate.'

He hesitated.

'Yes,' he said slowly. 'Art, I'm afraid is a quixotic business. But then no one has ever pretended that the artist is really sane.'

'Isn't there something rather important in insanity?'

'Mm – Yes. Provided that you're sane periodically.'

Barbara's eyes are turned to one of her father's favourite paintings, which had never achieved critical acclaim:

She looked up at the 'Genius of Warfare', so that his eyes followed the direction of hers and rested, with hers, on the little card which said defiantly. 'Rejected. 1922.'

'Isn't that important?' she asked, nodding at the soldier's strange piercing eyes. More important than anything else?'

'Yes,' he said.

The novel had its popularity, though not within the walls of Monkton Combe where Huntersfield was quickly seen as a parody of Monkton. Indeed, the Secretary of the Old Monktonian Club suggested that the school governors should have been consulted before publication. R.C.H. would have taken pleasure in one reviewer's observation that 'the pictures of girls' school life hit the mark too incredibly accurately to come from the pen of a man'. Clearly Margaret's experience contributed considerably to this evocation.

R.C.H.'s parents must have had a generous sense of humour to appreciate the book's portrayal of evangelicalism, for it was to them that R.C.H. dedicated the novel. But perhaps he was really offering to them what is the underlying tone of the work – a sympathetic understanding of religious convictions, the extremes of which the author himself could not embrace, but the genuine nature of which, and the courage in which they were held, he never doubted. It remained a novel for which he had great affection.

Rupert Hart-Davis described the first two novels in military terms as 'sighting shots', and R.C.H. had the conviction from his teen days that he had within him the imaginative breadth to create the 'grand' novel. He wanted to share the stage with the narrative dramas of writers such as Tolstoy and Thackeray (an author for whom he was developing an increasing respect). He later suggested, in 1949, that most novels gain by being contained within 100,000 words, but he had by then exceeded this total four times. The background for such a possible canvas (which he now had in mind) was that of war, which would enable him to explore the internal conflicts of his characters played out against the external conflicts of military action. In the early 1930s one obvious setting for such a narrative was the horrific political state of continental Europe in the early 1920s, and in particular the fragile, often hostile relationship simmering between England and Germany.

His idea began to form into the shape of a novel set in three parts – one in England, one in Germany, and one bringing the two together. Each country would evoke opposite poles of atmosphere. The first, in England, painting a world of languid, self-confidence; a world of comfortable security, of aristocratic pleasures in horse riding, country cricket, and the 'gentlemanly' sport of rugby football; a social life revolving around dining and pipe-smoking in the homely atmosphere of armchairs in village pubs, surrounded by faded prints on the wall:

> the places where gentlemen lived, away from the restless stirring of new societies called Trade Unions. There had been a fear that our furious progress would carry us into an unaccustomed world. But the world remained to let us enjoy peacefully our sense of accomplishment. Horses pulled tramway-carts through the streets of Cambridge, but the postman still came across the fields on foot from the village to the Rectory. The garden slept between its high, brown walls, Cragg moved his barrow another yard and let it rest again, and sitting in his padded desk-chair my father spoke to his sons about the honour of a gentleman, about the romantic emotions of young women, about dangerous intimacy, about the rank of our forbears, the clock above him ticking domestically as the words fell out from the fathers' book of all the centuries.

The German world would be the opposite – a country torn to pieces by a war which was far from over in mental and emotional terms, and far from peaceful within towns filled with violent unrest, inhabited by lawless, starving deserters, anarchists, and vagabonds, camping in crumbling evacuated buildings, with threatening faces staring from broken windows, and the crack of sniper fire the only sound by night.

This was to form the framework of his third, and far more adventurous novel (covering more than 500 pages), *The Unforgotten Prisoner*. Its publication transformed the possible breadth of R.C.H.'s imaginative landscape. It received a warm public reception, selling 150,000 copies in the first month, was recommended by the Book Society, and went into immediate editions in America and Canada, and received German, Dutch, and Hungarian translations. Encouraging praise came from Compton Mackenzie, calling it 'the best English novel that has been published this year, and one of the half-dozen best English novels written since the war'. He also described the 'symphonic construction' of the novel producing 'the kind of novel that I feel Beethoven would have appreciated'. This construction required decisions about narration – an element which R.C.H. liked to experiment with in almost every novel. He uses, in this case, two narrators: the middle section is provided by a nameless voice; the other sections are told by John Saggard, a young son of a snobbish, financially secure country vicar. We follow Saggard's journey from before, during, and post war. He enjoys all the pleasures of country life, and the description of a village cricket match is as amusing as that famously described by A.G. Macdonell in *England Their England* (published in the same month as *The Unforgotten Prisoner*).

Saggard provides the backdrop to the major thematic strands of the novel – the war itself, the effects of war on survivors, the personal relationships between English and German individuals, and the mental disturbance of a young boy brought up with all these factors intruding on his growing years. One has to keep reminding oneself that R.C.H. was writing this in his twenties, with no experience of war.

Saggard is at the heart of the problems of English-German interaction. It stems from his pre-war home life, where the family's au pair is a young German girl, Hedwig, who elopes with Saggard's brother, Charles, but the intervention of war results in the break-up of the relationship and Hedwig (now pregnant, unbeknown to Charles) returns to Germany and marries Heinrich, who becomes 'father' to Hedwig's son, Klaus, who is unaware of his biological father. Saggard, during the war, becomes responsible for overseeing the execution of Heinrich, who, posing as an American soldier, is uncovered as a German spy, and Saggard later discovers the true identity of Heinrich and the existence of Klaus, though he keeps this information from Charles. He is deeply troubled by his role in the execution of Heinrich and secretly follows the career of Klaus.

The figure of Klaus takes centre stage. He is the first of many troubled minds to occupy prime position in R.C.H.'s novels, and he is one of the most memorable. It is a gruelling experience to follow his journey of deepening mental turmoil. His mother has sent him to a seminary where he is brutally inculcated with religious fanaticism – Roman Catholic this time, instead of evangelical. Within the Abbey Walls, the same worries about extreme Catholicism came to a sensitive monk as came to the schoolboy Hutchinson about fervent evangelicalism: Brother Peter, looking at the faces of the boys passing him for benediction, picks out one with 'eyes puckered and nearly closed, lips turned down; a fighter, Brother Peter thought, but no love, no love, no *love*'. Being a wanderer by nature Klaus is deeply traumatised by being incarcerated in the Abbey's 'Penitence Chamber' for striking a fellow student. As heralded by the title of the novel, Klaus becomes a prisoner in a variety of confinements: in the cellar of a food store and in a deserted piano factory, more like an asylum, occupied by a band of fanatical and dangerously unstable revolutionaries. He lives with a recurring horror of losing his liberty and this is always symbolised by the image of the Penitence Chamber. In his frantic escape from the Abbey he finds himself in a dark claustrophobic railway tunnel. It is the grimmest setting for his worst nightmare:

> He looked to right and left. Yes, if he stood with his back against the wall of the tunnel there should be just enough room for him to keep clear of a passing train – he was not sure how far it bulged over the lines. But it was not the train that he feared. The rush of a train was only like the sweep of a boy's fist, swifter, fiercer, more final, to be dodged or suffered. He had no fear of hard loud-sounding things. It was the tunnel itself, the wall sweeping right over, the end stopped by a hollow, black nothingness. If he could only think of himself as a being progressing steadily along a tube from one day-lit country to another he would be alright. But he was afraid he might forget. The interval was so short, the likeness so great. Only the sleepers and rails – differing

little enough from the other hard things, a hard bench, or a cold, smooth tumbler – were there to remind him that he was not back again, shut in, with the door locked and the window high above reach, in the ghostly darkness of the Penitence Chamber. Or back still farther to something that was only a shape, a colour in his dimmest memory, a prison where someone wanted him to die. Wanted him to die. He knew that now. The tunnel, the room, the prison where someone wanted him to die. And if someone tipped up the tube, so that the emptiness came beneath him... He began to lose all faith, almost to forget that there was a world of green hills with the sun shining; and the ghostly, paralysing thoughts pressed harder. He pictured the train again, forced it, as he sweated, to appear before his closed eyes, until he became one with it and thought that he was an engine, a bulk of inanimate ferocity rushing through a tunnel that had no power to restrain a thing so huge and mighty. On, still running, still thrusting back the invading horrors, still faintly hoping that when he opened his eyes the darkness would have vanished. But he dared not open them, could not face the reality of utter blindness.

Klaus's real prison, however, is his own mind. He becomes more unpredictable and violent as the novel develops. Everyone he meets and everything he encounters becomes a challenge to his sense of a desire for freedom. He is slowly disintegrating into 'Klaus, a dead thing, an animal with no mentality beyond the uprush of crazy emotions'. Being reunited with his mother, who is fast losing hold on reality, he is indoctrinated into believing that all English people are evil and to be distrusted: 'They killed your Father!' He eventually sets fire to his mother's house while she is inside, and later sets fire to the piano factory – but has no clear memory of either event, nor can he express any motive. The bleak description of him holding the body of his dead mother in his arms is as black a picture of mental suffering as could be painted:

He was quick enough to save her, breaking his own fall with his left arm, catching her about the shoulders with his right. When the shock had passed he turned to see her face. Her head hung loose, the skin of her throat taut with its weight.

He shifted his arm and her head rolled over sideways; got
up, and she was lying on the floor as if pitched there from
a hunter's spear. So that was what had been happening!
He thought now that he had half-suspected it, could not
apprehend a culmination of the bitter apartness. Someone
had taken a pair of scissors, waited until he was drowsy, and
snipped through the central cord inside his head; he could
feel the loose end hanging, dripping. Back in the Penitence
Chamber.

There are moments of brightness – Klaus takes pride in his
mechanical ability, repairing the engine of the car of one kindly
monk at the Abbey, and later showing his skills as a mechanic in a
London car workshop (echoes of Khamhaiv); we hear the violin
melody played by one of the freedom fighters in the piano factory, a
sound which resounds in the memory long after the fire. He enjoys a
brief period of inner calm when walking purposefully through the
countryside in the company of a young girl, Berta. He confides to her:

> 'I'm not going back', he said, 'not going back, however
> much they want me. I like to be where there are no
> walls' … 'Berlin's nice,' he continued. 'But I shan't go back
> there either. We had a lovely garden, but I don't remember it
> very well. If you go back you have to go through all the other
> places, back through the railway tunnel, through the Abbey.
> I'd rather go straight on.'

But he even leaves Berta, to go 'straight on' through Holland and
eventually to England, where he is 'adopted' by Saggard, whose history
remains unknown to Klaus. After much suspicion from Klaus a kind
of relationship is formed between them, though probably stronger on
Saggard's side than Klaus's.

It seems that Klaus can never escape from his memories of
confinement and associated terror. When a friend of Saggard's asks
him what he dreams about he replies: 'Things I do not care about.
A Penitence Chamber and a piano factory.' Once again there is a
definitive incident in an art studio. Saggard's artist friend, Elaine, has
befriended Klaus, and painted a picture entitled 'A Boy Laughing',
which was later to hang in Saggard's house. Saggard wonders if Klaus
was the model:

The figure was that of a boy naked to the waist, his legs covered by loose, ragged trousers, the shadow of the fishing boat falling across his bare feet, which I saw, when I looked closely, were a man's feet, big and bony. You could see, when you stopped feeling the picture and started to study it, that the boy had just come out of the cave, where he had been sleeping. His eyes were strained, meeting the fierce sunshine that glistened on his strong, young body. His arms were bent up at the elbows, his fingers pressed into his palms, his shoulders bent back. His chin was uptilted a little. He was not laughing, only about to laugh; so near to it that you wanted to pull a face at him to set him roaring... The poise, the freshness of his body, the curious, opening mouth, held my eyes as they were generally held only by the finest sculpture. They touched me in an emotion that was beyond the emotion of beauty suddenly perceived.

Saggard asked Elaine how Klaus reacted to the picture. She said she was confused by his reaction: 'He pointed to the cave and said "like a Penitence Chamber!" and laughed ... then he got frightfully serious again and stood gazing at the thing as if it was something by Picasso and saying: "Very fine! Very fine! *Herrlich!* Magnificent!"'

But Klaus's wanderlust is untamed and the last we see of him is his embarking on another journey, to join Berta in Germany. The final parting takes place in R.C.H.'s favourite setting, a railway station.

Saggard's affection for Klaus might well include some self-desire to expiate his own sense of guilt, but he sees a nobility within Klaus's suffering which becomes a symbol for all the ambiguous feelings that war has engendered within Saggard himself. As he leaves the station, he falteringly explains these feeling to his wife:

'We loved him because he was a kind person. I don't think he'd ever have been unkind, not purposely. When I think of him I think of his eyes, and his lips smiling. It hurts, but when it hurts I see him more clearly. It becomes – fixed in me, part of me. You know, there were men in the war I remember like that. It used to hurt so much I tried not to think about them. But I knew they'd been kind, they'd always been decent, you felt the kindness even when they'd been ripped into fragments by the shrapnel. They'd added something to

life. I think that's what – makes the thing worth it. People add
something. They get something given them as a sort of seed –
I think they get it from Galilee – and they add something,
and they suffer, and it piles up. You can't see it all, but you feel
the weight of it, driving against cruelty and evil … It's beauty,'
I said wildly, 'it goes on like a flame, it can't perish.'

This conviction that hope can come from despair is to mark the
conclusion of all R.C.H.'s novels, though with varying degrees of
assurance. An early possible title for the novel was *Towards Morning*
and each word is heavy with possible interpretive suggestions: light
will eventually emerge from the darkness of night, however mistily
(there *are* 'green hills with the sun shining' at the end of Klaus's tunnel),
but the telling word is 'Towards' – for R.C.H., resolution is always a
progression, a future possibility, and it is the journey 'towards' the
horizon which engages his imagination. One remembers 'A Boy
Laughing': 'He was not laughing. Only about to laugh.' As Klaus's
train leaves the platform he is starting 'towards' a potentially brighter
life, certainly in a more stable mental state than when he arrived, but
we never see him at his destination. His future happiness, if granted,
lies hidden in the novel's unwritten chapter. The first two words of
the *actual* final chapter are indeed, 'Towards morning'. Yet again,
one's mind returns to the schoolboy red book, which offers a view of
a realistic path to happiness, in very Hutchinsonian tones: 'We must
hold the torch, we *must* keep love, but we must plunge full of hope
into the darkness. This sounds rhetorical; but I think it is true.'

The same sort of duality lies within the novel's title – *who* is the
'unforgotten prisoner'? In terms of simple narrative it would be
Heinrich, the only actual physical prisoner, but the title also embraces
those whom war has emotionally confined – Saggard, Hedwig, and
ultimately Klaus. None of these will ever be 'forgotten' by the reader.

After its initial enthusiastic reception, *The Unforgotten Prisoner*
waited until 1983 for a second English edition – a pattern that
was to become all too familiar in the mercurial history of R.C.H.'s
publications. The new edition was welcomed by *The Times Literary
Supplement* with an acutely perceptive review by Valentine
Cunningham. Like most reviewers of R.C.H., Cunningham was
confronted with the problem of describing a narrative which has
passages of extraordinary vividness, of deep human sympathy,
of suspense, of sadness, of light and darkness, often expressed in

haunting poetic prose. But he also finds these moments interwoven with R.C.H.'s excursions into extremes of descriptive exaggeration and emotional rhetoric. Cunningham points to the high achievements of a novel in which the author shows his 'deepest revulsion from the madness, turmoil and inhuman frenzies of European war, violent revolutions, violent politics of any sort'. He gives some glittering praise of R.C.H.'s descriptive powers at key moments:

> achieved with extraordinary skill and imaginative grasp … Hutchinson's football crowd is as good as Henry Greene's; his street scenes as good as John Sommerfield's; his awful school episodes are as oppressive as any of Graham Greene's … the satiric play the novel makes with the distressing chauvinism of the Empire-building British press … as telling as Auden's; his prisons and his *poesie de departs* as terrifying and poignant as anything in Conrad or Kafka.

He suggests that that the description of scenes at the piano factory read 'like something out of Dostoevsky'. But he also finds these excellent episodes marred by intrusions of sentimentality, melodrama, and 'scarcely credible coincidences', He wonders if Hutchinson had been reading too much Dickens.

Throughout his writing career, R.C.H. had reviewers who concentrated on these presumed 'weaknesses', accusing the author of becoming cliché-ridden, and too prone to the sentimental. Others pointed to such flaws but showed their frustration in finding that, far from detracting from the whole novel's narrative balance, they sometimes seemed to complement it. The opening chapter of *Great Expectations* could easily be accused of falling into these traps – levity mixed with tension; melodrama knocking on the door of cliché. Yet these pages catch the imagination of most of Dickens' readers. Perhaps R.C.H. had indeed been more influenced than he imagined when, at school, he was so entranced by the dramatic readings of Dickens by the Reverend Runnels-Moss, providing 'the jolliest day so far this term'.

An engaging expression of a reader's experience of being confronted by this mixture of narrative voices appeared in Lionel Hale's review of the first edition, on publication, in the *News Chronicle*:

> A very fine novel indeed! It is also extremely ill-planned; it is marred by mistimed levity; it begins by being founded

on improbability, it goes on by being much too long and it
ends by being obscure. I haven't enjoyed a novel so much
for months! ... Mr. Hutchinson has so many arrows, he
disdains a shield ... he has a mind, and its vigour and
clarity are stamped on every sentence he writes; he has
an eye and doesn't bother if there are motes in it. What a
novel! Full of holes as a sieve, it holds water.

It took 50 years for the posthumous review from Cunningham to
see comparisons (in what was only R.C.H.'s third published novel,
written in his early twenties) with Graham Greene, Auden, Conrad,
Kafka, Dostoevsky and Dickens. What encouragement that would
have given to R.C.H. in 1933, coming home to pick up his pen in his
modest flat in Norwich after a tedious day in the office.

Life was becoming increasingly busy, with Ann being joined by a
brother, Jeremy, in October 1932, and the family was to be completed
by the birth of Elspeth in June 1934 and Piers in August 1937. To add
to the preoccupations of domestic commitments, the encouraging
sales of *The Unforgotten Prisoner* instantly inspired R.C.H. with ideas
for further novels.

One might have thought that the next volume would follow the
pattern of *The Unforgotten Prisoner* and develop the landscape of war-
torn Europe, but R.C.H. – as was becoming a habit – immediately
decided to go in a quite different direction and leave the unfinished
business of *The Unforgotten Prisoner* until the fifth novel *Shining
Scabbard*. First, he put on his imaginative eyeglass to view a new and
unexpected landscape – the Siberian tundra.

The Answering Glory had explored spiritual courage, but in
One Light Burning R.C.H. extends the concept of exploration to
encompass physical and intellectual heroism – Andrew Wild, an
Oxford professor of philosophy, is convinced that his friend Franz
Grundmann, a German theologian, is the only person able to marry
metaphysics and theology but Grundmann has disappeared while
venturing into forbidden Siberian territory to distribute Bibles to
the dispersed inhabitants. Wild believes Grundmann is alive and
is determined to rescue him. The novel paints vivid descriptions
of Wild's challenging journey by foot and sledge across the ice and
snow, conditions deteriorating by the day. He is eventually left alone
(having lost his fellow travellers from frostbite or fatigue), except
for one companion who is losing his mind and has to be dragged

by Wild (now exhausted and confused) across the bleak, freezing
tundra. R.C.H. had, of course, no personal knowledge of the Arctic,
but achieves memorable evocations of an imagined landscape:

> They rounded the bend and came into a straight piece,
> running at least a mile before the right bank swung round
> to cut it off. It was Andrew, then, who could have sworn
> against his reason that they had covered that very stretch
> earlier in the day. But why? There was no landmark, save
> the trunk of a larch which rested on its passage to the sea,
> oddly and precariously held by an out-jutting hump of
> rock. The banks were low here, and mounted in the bows
> on a tea-box he could see, with a turn of his head, the whole
> extent of the tundra as far as eyesight would carry, dun-
> coloured, flecked with iron-grey and patches of dull green,
> meshed widely by the courses of vanished streams, without
> trees, without live grass, without boundaries. At this hour
> the light was very clear. The wind, cold and damp against
> his skin, still blew from the same quarter, unchanged in
> velocity, not in sharp and wilful currents, but as a continent
> of air advancing in unhindered motion across the earth's
> easy surface; dustless, and carrying no cloud, leaving the
> steady fall of light untroubled by its gigantic progress. From
> above, like the summer sky of Italy reflected in deep, still
> water, vaporous but taut-stretched and motionless, the sky
> curved down to the limit of the eye's reach and kept pace,
> itself unmoving, with the creeping shutava, so that the
> boat's wriggle along the twisted, flowing river seemed to
> win no advancement. Only the water moved; the landscape
> was fixed, a picture done by a painter with a sense of tones
> but none of arrangement or perspective. The movement of
> the banks, bending, rising and falling a little, widening and
> narrowing, seemed only a flattery, a counterfeit of covered
> distances. Another day half-gone, with no change, nothing
> to mark accomplishment.

The reader may well be puzzled by what is being referred to as
'shutava', and R.C.H.'s desire to create realistic portrayals of places
he had never visited, or to invent local words, is sometimes taken to
extremes in *One Light Burning*, as fact and fantasy play with each

other. Those readers who are familiar with Warsaw may have no
problems with following the characters crossing the Poniatowskiego
Bridge or visiting the Plac Tetralny, but no atlas will help the reader
to place Osyefta, Gostkeff, Tel Rak, or the Stavonoi mountains. And
what are Niutchas, nartas – or shutava?

Back in firm reality, however, Wild has more than one quest, for
his search for Grundmann is joined by a romantic one. Although
considered a confirmed bachelor, Wild has fallen desperately in love
with a young bride, Greta, and follows her both before and after his
Arctic adventure. Each quest seems doomed to failure – Wild fails
to find Grundmann in the tundra and seems permanently separated
from the married Greta.

But there is yet another strand to weave into these criss-crossing
hopes and hurdles. R.C.H.'s interest and exploration of psychological
and physical abnormalities increases and develops in each novel.
The amusing and poignant portrayal of 'beautiful insanity' in *The
Answering Glory* is a springboard for the grimmer mental distress
of Klaus. In Wild we are given an analytical case-history of acute
insomnia. His inability to sleep leads him to the verges of nervous
breakdown as he is forced to cope with mental fatigue exacerbating
physical exhaustion. The novel's title brings these elements together
and is taken from a poem of Siegfried Sassoon:

> *You that keep*
> *In a land of sleep*
> *One light burning till break of day.*

The novel moves between these two poetic concepts of light and
sleep. There are at least a hundred references to these two contrasting
yet equally powerful motifs: love is almost always accompanied by
light; despair by sleeplessness. This interplay is captured in a moment
on board ship, when Wild feels an early desire for Greta as she,
symbolically, moves between light and shadow while Wild's reason
'slumbered':

> She had moved away from the light, then, and he could no
> longer see her except as a coated form in the shadow. He
> would have liked to stretch out and feel her hand to see
> if it were cold again, but something prevented him. Not
> prudence, for his reason slumbered. Franz was distant in

his mind, farther than Franz had been since the voyage started; and the moment in which he lived was cut off from the past and future by an enchantment he would not break with sound or movement. It was enough by itself to satisfy his spirit and his senses. Even the pity of it was dear to him; a flame, live and scorching, which kindled an emotion he had not learnt before, richer and more tender than all the colours of his experience, releasing a new power, bringing warmth to every vein of his consciousness. The night breeze, colder but still gentle, blew across his face, and he felt it as time flowing past him, drifting as the coast-lights drifted while they two stood, motionless, neither closer nor farther from each other, as the unbroken moment stretched out to hold them. It was a stranger beside him, her body in shadow and her soul hidden deeply. But he could keep her there, till time intervening caught and dragged them forward, by his own quiescence, by the strength of his pity. He thought they were two figures carved one of bronze and one of marble; like marble, her face light in the shadow against the dark colour of his coat; sculptured by the same artist, sold to different buyers, placed at last – by chance and carelessly – together in a corner of a deserted gallery; turned to face each other, to gaze for ever with eyes carved blind upon living faces, one suffering and the other pitiful. There, in that still gallery, with the noises of the street's traffic subdued by the intervening quietness, they would stand untroubled by the impudent gaze of sightseers.

The question remains as to how many of Wild's quests end in resolution. He does, in fact, have renewed contact with Grundmann, whom he presumed was dead. But his precarious nervous state leaves him puzzled as to whether this reunion is real or an illusion. Has his journey been one of heroic fulfilment or heroic failure? He is finally together with Greta, but is wracked with guilt that he might have been responsible for the death of her husband. The last tableau is that of Wild, silent and distracted, but in Greta's arms: 'His head had sunk on Greta's shoulder, his face turned up. His eyes were closed, a little colour had come into his cheeks. His mouth was parted slightly, his breathing deep and even. He was fast asleep.'

Wild was not the only person travelling simultaneously in different directions, for R.C.H. was planning *Shining Scabbard* while he was still at work on *One Light Burning*, and there were only sixteen months between the publication of each (and *Shining Scabbard* was considerably longer). It is remarkable that he could keep two such different worlds in his imagination at the same time – the wastelands of the sparsely populated Arctic live together with the world of a small French town, Baulon l'Epais, waiting agonisingly for the first shots of war. R.C.H.'s evocation of the tundra was drawn entirely from second-hand sources, but in *Shining Scabbard* he captures the everyday smells, sights and sounds of a provincial French town with a penetrating realism that suggests first-hand knowledge – but he had never been to France. He was delighted to receive a letter from the office of his agents, Curtis Brown: 'It is incomprehensible to me that anyone could write *Shining Scabbard* without an intimate knowledge of the French family point of view, for when I read the book, I felt certain that you knew the French and their ways through long association', and another admirer observed that 'he writes in English but he thinks in French'.

The two novels are also vastly different in tone as well as setting. *One Light Burning* is in essence a novel of psychological dissection, with little surface humour. Two reviewers suggested that the figure of Conrad was hovering over R.C.H.'s shoulders. *Shining Scabbard* is a novel dealing with the grim world of a community waiting nervously for military action, but the tone (until the end) is predominantly humorous in its portrayal of human eccentricity, and one feels that R.C.H.'s schoolboy hero, Dickens, is a regular visitor to his creative world. The life of Baulon l'Epais is centred on the Séverin household, a family of absurdly self-obsessed individuals, headed by the old, infirm, former soldier Eugène Séverin, totally concerned with clearing his name, having been accused of cowardice and desertion of the battlefield many years before. The court case dealing with this (the 'Séverin affair') has dragged on even longer than 'Jarndyce and Jarndyce' in Dickens' *Bleak House* (and R.C.H. returns to protracted legal disputes in *Image of My Father*). Séverin's room is surrounded by battle maps of the incident, which he studies daily from his sick room. He is a natural successor to Uncle Toby in Sterne's *Tristram Shandy* and even more of a hypochondriac than Mr Woodhouse in Austen's *Emma*. The family extends to Eugène's sister, crippled with rheumatism, who sees herself as the real head of the family, and always hopes to return to her 'salad days' when she was, in her eyes, a doyen of the Paris theatre decades before. With a feeble wife, an horrific aged mother (quite insane), who imagines herself to be on a perpetual hunting expedition across the fields of the French countryside, Eugène's household is also inhabited by a constantly ill-tempered housekeeper with an imbecile son.

The novel consists, mostly, of a series of comic tableaux as the Séverin family play out their ludicrous roles, which makes the narrative become focused on characterisation rather than plot. An incident in a solicitor's office, where the family are trying to interview a vital witness in the 'Séverin affair', for whom they have been searching for many years, takes over thirteen pages of description in which the various characters manage not to communicate with each other but only express their own obsessions in comic exchanges – and the witness turns out to be a drunkard who has no precise memory of the original events. Gradually the madness within the family becomes more manic and macabre: the elderly grandmother, in one of her angry fits, extinguishes her cigarette on her son's cheek in the middle of an otherwise humorous conversation, and there is a scene of black humour in a discussion of an unsuccessful attempt to euthanize the family dog. These are sure signs that the novel is moving from tragic-comedy to something more inherently disturbing. The words of a more mentally stable member of the Séverin family, Eugène's younger son Raymond, portray the family acutely:

> They know nothing of what is going on, they are wholly occupied with their own concerns, with the eternal 'Affaire Séverin' which everyone else in the world has forgotten. Really, it's a relief to be with people who are plainly ignorant instead of those whose ignorance is diluted by epidemic funk into a liquid soup of poisonous garrulity.

A perceptive reviewer observed that the Séverin family is 'a microcosm of a nation's madness in a world going out of its head'.

Introduced into this dysfunctional family is a figure of sanity, Renée, the wife of Eugène's elder son Pierre. She is living in the household with her daughter and son – Armand, a troubled boy, seemingly autistic and owing much to the portrait of Klaus in *The Unforgotten Prisoner*. Renée is living in misery, only sustained by the hope of the return of Pierre, who has followed in the family tradition and has deserted from the army in Africa in order to be united with his family and defend his country against the Prussians. R.C.H. was intensely drawn to the ethical problems surrounding 'desertion' and it becomes an issue in later novels. Under arrest, Pierre offers a solution to his thoughtful interrogator, Bouheyre, and suggests that, if a pistol was placed on the table, 'I'd waste precious little more of your time!' Bouheyre declines to do so, but argues with himself (including R.C.H.'s favourite word, 'guts'):

> He cursed Séverin, putting him through this, just when he was up to the eyes. But the guts of the fellow! No one but a madman like Séverin would ever have dreamed of such an escapade. And now they would shoot him for cowardice. Yes, it was inevitable that France was pitting its forces against those of a nation twice as large, that bravery was worth everything that the professors of Saint-Cyr had ever written in the text- books … that would count for nothing against the formal conception of military discipline, the system, the dogma of obedience … Yes, they'd keep Séverin and question him and maul him about, they wouldn't listen to a word of his explanation, they'd parade his peccadilloes once again before the bulging eyes of the proletariat and then with appropriate pantomimery they'd put half a dozen bullets in his chest. Séverin himself was right: it would save everyone's time if Bouheyre was careless enough to leave his Mauser on the table.

Pierre sets out on a typical Hutchinsonian journey to return to Renée, which includes the pretence of being a corpse, as he travels by foot, train, motor, and canoe. Renée , who has never been fully accepted by the Séverin family because of her dark-coloured skin (she is referred to, behind her back, as 'that mulatto'), waits patiently for Renée's safe return.

As the sounds of warfare resound around the town, the inhabitants of Baulon are instructed to evacuate but Eugène refuses to leave as he believes he has been appointed by headquarters in Paris to lead the military defence of the town against the Prussians. He is waiting for a telegram to give him orders to go ahead.

There is one other figure of sanity among all the confusion, and as so often in the novels it is a doctor – the humane and ever-caring Dr Tischer. While he is tending a desperately ill man, he is arrested by the police, for though he has ministered to Baulon for most of his life, he is Swiss by origin. When rescuing a baby from a house destroyed by Prussian firing, he is turned on by the local inhabitants and clubbed to death as 'one of the enemy'.

Pierre and Renée are finally reunited with their children, but when rushing for shelter in a cellar during a sniper attack, they realise that Armand is left outside. Renée rushes to save him but both are shot down by Prussian shells. Pierre stands over the bodies of his wife and son but 'he did not look at them for long, he could not manage that'. What he did see was that 'they lay face to face, and so close that their fingers touched, as if they understood each other'.

Both of the novels received immediate success, both in Britain and in America and R.C.H.'s popularity in the States initiated one of his rare excursions abroad in 1948, when he visited New York with much enjoyment. *One Light Burning* became the best-selling novel in England for two consecutive weeks and was a Book-of-the-Month recommendation in the USA (as was *Shining Scabbard*) which added the potential of a further 50,000 copies. Reviews of *One Light Burning* included claims that R.C.H. was 'the best male novelist his generation has produced in England' and 'Definitely, Mr. Hutchinson is competing with the giants of literature'. An eloquent New York reviewer captured what was becoming the mark of a Hutchinsonian conclusion to a novel – the 'one light burning', Saggard's 'flame' that 'can't perish': 'In this day and time it is startling to find a novelist of ability whose hero is pure idealist, whose theme is vaguely spiritual, whose country of the soul reveals a blankness like that of the Siberian steppes – yet who finally leaves readers with a sensation of hope in eternal things.' *Shining Scabbard's* sales were even better, reaching 78,000 copies in America alone in the first two weeks. An American reviewer claimed it as 'the best Anglo-Saxon portrait of a French family since Henry James's *The American*'. Looking back with an objective eye thirteen years later, R.C.H. modestly recorded: 'This was probably the tidiest novel I have done – it has, I think, fewer technical blunders than the others – but it was fatally lacking in philosophical implications of any kind: it poses no problem concerned with the opposition of good and evil.' This was not something that seemed to worry the reading public at the time of publication. In 1936, he must have taken particular pleasure in the opinion of two fellow novelists: Edith Wharton described it as 'A strange, fantastic, irresistible novel' and Pamela Hansford Johnson found it 'An exceptionally fine book, so surely conceived, so remarkably executed, that it should take its place, not only among the novels of the year, but of the century.'

The success of these four early novels had a significant practical benefit, as Cassells offered an advance of £500 for each of the next four. This financial security and signs of confidence in his literary talent enabled R.C.H. and Margaret to take the plunge and allowed R.C.H. to escape from his desk at Colman's and rent a cottage at Birdlip, 1,000 feet up in the Cotswolds, where they could have room for Ann, Jeremy and Elspeth (now ranging in age from 2 to nearly 6). King's Head Cottage, a former public house, had a romantic air – R.C.H. drew an attractive sketch of it – though it was not full of mod-cons: the only water supply was what fell on the roof and was collected in an underground tank.

To extend Rupert Hart-Davis's description of the first two novels as 'sighting shots', the next three moved in terms of structure and narrative balance ever nearer the inner ring. R.C.H. could now enjoy his own family home, though his real home was his study – his daily creative retreat – which was to be the cradle for his first literary 'bullseye': *Testament*. He had now achieved his boyhood ambition, he was a 'professional writer'. He was just 28 years old.

R.C.H. (right) about to fly off.
Oxford Air Squadron.

King's Head Cottage, Birdlip. Sketch by R.C.H.

R.C.H. and children, Piers, Elspeth, Jeremy and Ann,
1939.

Chapter 4

The Writer at his Desk

There may well be a fascinating study to be written describing authors' choices of atmosphere in which they choose to create their work – the amount of space in which they felt relaxed, the furniture they liked to be surrounded by (especially their choice of desk) – and how these choices give insights into their individual creative imaginations, either by contrast or imitation. One thinks of the spacious, cluttered study of Ray Bradbury, so crammed that a desk is scarcely visible, but which inspired the vision of single individuals in *Fahrenheit 451* who could hold a complete novel within their minds without requiring any external stimulus. F. Scott Fitzgerald squeezed himself into a cramped space where there was hardly any room to write, providing the claustrophobic and emotional intensity of *The Great Gatsby*. By contrast, Hemingway chose a large, almost empty room and worked at a table more likely to be found in a kitchen. The floor of Dylan Thomas' hut was littered with discarded crumpled pages of rejected drafts of poetic lines. Thackeray's simple, small, plain table, with no drawers, produced the broad vision of *Vanity Fair*. Dickens preferred a desk, usually with sloping top, full of drawers (possibly crammed with random notes and observations), but significantly liked a study with a mirror in which he could distort his facial features until he found a suitable facial expression for one of his caricatures. Jane Austen's simple, round occasional table enabled her to pretend that she was not writing at all. Trollope liked to stand at his writing desk, like a lectern, as though there was no time to be lost before the office opened. On the other hand, Roald Dahl liked the comfort of a high-backed armchair and wrote on a single-legged stool like a hospital side-table. Robert Frost disdained a table altogether and wrote, in a comfortable chair, on what looks like an orchestral violin stand, as though writing a letter to his readers. At another extreme we see J.D. Salinger sitting naked on a packing case, his typewriter precariously balanced on the opened trunk at the rear of his motor van. The list is endless...

What then can we learn from the surroundings which R.C.H. chose to stimulate his imagination? For, except for wartime interruptions, his study was to be his daily inner sanctuary whenever possible. How acutely prophetic the opening sentence of his schoolboy diary was: 'my life consists, I think, more in thought than in deed'.

One important caveat needs to be emphasised before attempting to picture R.C.H. at his desk: it would be a mistake to imagine him as some sort of recluse. His friends knew him to be shy by nature, but when he was relaxed he was an engaging, warm, and witty companion. He did not feel at home in what he called the literary world: 'I've never been in the literary world. The mere smell of it in *The Observer* daunts me', but he was elected as a Fellow of the Royal Society of Literature in 1962, and reluctantly accepted a variety of invitations to speak at literary events, including the Irish branch of PEN, and the Association of Yorkshire Bookmen, and gave speeches in 1965 at the dinner of the Society of Civil Service Authors and at the annual lunch of the English Association, but admitted that 'such chores terrify me. It is only a lamentable weakness of mind that lets me in for them.' He preferred smaller occasions, especially those of local societies closer to home, giving talks at the Cheltenham Literary Society in 1938 and ten years later to the Farnham Women's Institute. He obviously had a gift for engaging an audience, receiving a letter from the BBC after a radio interview on being awarded the W.H. Smith Literary Award, congratulating him on being 'one of the best interviewees that had been heard for a long time'. A sure sign of his sociability within small groups was his pleasure in being a member of the Garrick Club (and clubs feature in a few of his short stories and in the opening of *Thou Hast A Devil*), before he resigned because of the expense. He wrote in 1973: 'I love the Garrick – it still seems to me the most civilized of clubs ... A cosy place, I think, with a certain modest elegance; and the servants are *so* nice – gentle and dignified and friendly. Moreover the cooking is now absolutely first-class.' His descriptions of Old Monktonian social events also show that he was much happier being in the audience at public events than being at 'top table'. In general, his remarks to his friend the poet Martyn Skinner summarised his vision of a perfect working life: 'How I love weeks when absolutely *nothing* happens (except the arrival of people I like).'

His desire to distance himself from the literary scene may seem a recipe for critical and commercial isolation, and his assertion that he 'never made allowances for my reader' may have a suicidal ring of indifference to his public popularity. But he was as conscious of the extent of his readership as any other author and especially since he had chosen to rely on his writing for his income. He was, however, determined to remain faithful to his own inner imaginative world, to tread his own solitary path, convinced that he had a unique vision which would always find a sympathetic audience, however numerically fluctuating and erratic that audience might be.

He worked mainly in three studies. At the end of 1938, he moved from Birdlip to the village of Crondall in Hampshire, on the edge of Farnham in Surrey. A rare emergence of the Coryton snobbery is evident in his desire to refer to Crondall as on the border of Hampshire rather than in Surrey. The house (known as Triggs) was a spacious home set in an acre of garden and orchard, with no near neighbours. Seventeen years later he moved to Bletchingley, an attractive village in Surrey, with medieval buildings set on an escarpment of the Greensand Ridge, and remained there for the rest of his life. R.C.H. usually preferred to use the old spelling of Blechingley rather than the modern spelling, Bletchingley.

The importance he placed on the geographical origins of the composition of each novel is clear in his habit of recording, on the final page, where each book was written. If the composition covered a period between moves, the appropriate dates would be carefully recorded, as in the case of *March the Ninth*:

- Crondall, 1955
- Bletchingley, 1957

and on the publication of *Elephant and Castle*, more specifically recording the process of the composition (and insisting again that Crondall was in Hampshire):

- Crondall, Hampshire
- Designed 1940
- Written 1945-48

The study at Crondall was on the first floor with a large beam crossing the ceiling. From here he could look out from one set of windows onto the front lawn and across a lane to a stream and fields beyond. Other windows revealed a barn and stables. It was a perfect oasis, and he installed a green-beige door to cover the original door, which shielded him from the inevitable noise of four children. His desk was uncluttered – just paper, inkwell, and a few books (certainly no typewriter). He banished the telephone to a small windowless room on the ground floor. He kept to a rigid almost military routine, with mornings, whenever possible, kept sacred to the study. Lunch was at a set time, followed by a period given over to the family before a return to the study. After a more relaxed supper, the study called again, though he would later be joined by Margaret. The same kind of pattern was followed on the move to Bletchingley (to a smaller house, Dysart, more suitable now some of the children had left home), writing in the mornings and evenings and spending afternoons walking and gardening. Triggs produced three full novels (*Interim* being mostly written in a wartime bedsitter in London) and half of two others; Dysart was the home for five full novels and the completion of a sixth. R.C.H. was at this time suffering from some back pain and in the Dysart study he erected a shelf on his desk so that he could read without bending his shoulders, and also made use of a kind of dais so that he could compose while standing.

The study walls were typically book-lined. After his death the books were dispersed, so it is impossible accurately to record all the volumes, but of some we can be certain – mostly extensions of the authors and areas recorded in his school reading and referred to in his correspondence: Thackeray, classic seventeenth-, eighteenth-, and nineteenth-century novelists, French novelists and philosophers (Balzac, Hugo, Zola, Proust, Descartes, and Pascal), and Russians (in particular Tolstoy and Dostoyevsky), and Conrad and Dickens must surely have been represented.

Especially interesting is the variety of reference books, for the most intriguing aspect of R.C.H.'s unique imagination is his ability to create entirely convincing evocations and closely observed descriptions of places he had never visited. We have seen that readers of *Shining Scabbard* assumed detailed personal knowledge of provincial France, even suspecting he had been a resident, and descriptions of Siberian tundra in *One Light Burning* appeared written from personal

experience. Rupert Hart-Davis, described being 'bowled over' by
reading *The Unforgotten Prisoner*:

> this long and appalling story of poverty and dereliction in
> the defeated Germany of 1919 must, I imagined, have been
> written by a man who had served in the British Army of
> Occupation and seen the horrors he so vividly described.
> Later I discovered that he had been eleven years old when
> the war ended.

More extraordinary, the huge canvas of Russia in *Testament* seemed
so real to many readers that Kate O'Brien remarked that it read as
though written by a Russian, and an English nurse who had worked
in Russia during the revolution wrote to R.C.H. about one episode
saying that they must have been on the same train. He explained that
at the time of the revolution he was 10 years old and that he had never
been further east than Warsaw. When asked how he achieved this
literary sleight of hand he was typically modest, claiming that it was
just a matter of routine research:

> I have been asked more than once how the knowledge of Rus-
> sia needed for the background of *Testament* was obtained.
> The answer is grievously simple. Municipal libraries contain
> many books by amateur travellers, naive autobiographers,
> excitable diarists and others, which are full of odd bits of
> information, available to anyone who will take the trou-
> ble to hunt them out. Background material is the least
> formidable of a novelist's difficulties; it involves donkey
> work, nothing more.

Such 'donkey work' took up many hours of searching through
documents and he was often surrounded by maps, postcards, phrase-
books, menus, and timetables, perusing them to achieve authenticity.
The reference section of the local library became a kind of second
study when he filled in the time between delivering his two younger children to primary school and picking them up later. His friend
Mervyn Horder, composer and chairman of Duckworth publishing
house, recalls being present when a niece of R.C.H.'s, resident in
Geneva, received a postcard asking her to check (for *A Child Possessed*)
the exact layout of the various passenger facilities on Geneva main

railway station. When Horder once expressed astonishment about the particularity of detail about obscure places in his novels, R.C.H. replied: 'Oh, well, that is what a novelist is for; if he can't do that, he can't do anything.' Some of the details, such as street names or titles of provincial newspapers are real, others imaginary, and it is often difficult to distinguish between the actual and the invented. In a letter to Martyn Skinner he made an interesting distinction between the acceptably 'imagined' and the acceptably 'invented' in a novel:

> Most of the native words in *March the Ninth* are genuine. But sobo-sabo is, as you have suspected … Hutch-balls. I *did* try. I spent, in fact, hours hunting for some game that might be played by cabin-boys in a Greek tramp; but I have not the British Museum close at hand, and in the end I surrendered … In my view a novelist must *not* – as I did in a very early book – put a lift into Monument tube-station, where some six million Englishmen know there is no lift. But if, in an English novel (as opposed to a work of Geography), I am 40% out in mentioning the distance in versts from Verkhoyansk to Oskogin, I do not care a hoot (even though I have had pages of reproof for just such errors from a don at Durham). Indeed, if I have characters travelling from V to O, and they are becoming unbearably tired or have run out of conversation, I will *deliberately* knock a hundred versts off the distance and cry boo to *all* the dons of Durham. But that is a species of original sin, from which I hope to be cured in time.

The novels may take the reader to Russia, Germany, France, Yugoslavia, and South America but they are more accurately located in the studies at King's Head Cottage, Triggs, and Dysart. As the editor of the journal *John Bull* acutely observed in February 1958, R.C.H. 'does his travelling in books'.

One volume would often be found on his desk and deserves special mention: Roget's *Thesaurus*, the popular reference book for those seeking synonyms of English words (it lists over 440,000 examples). R.C.H. must have been amused by Roget's explanation for the reason for its compilation, as Roget explains that he wished 'to hold out a helping hand … to those who are painfully groping their way and struggling with the difficulties of composition'. Certainly R.C.H.

seems obsessed with incorporating obscure vocabulary in his search
for just the right sense, and most readers must find Roget and a
dictionary useful companions when faced which such words as
griseous, stercoral, sciurine, uberty, urceolate, fuliginous, monticules,
and lincrusta. One assumes that Mervyn Horder had his tongue in
his cheek when remarking on R.C.H.'s use of 'outlandish epithets' and
then describing R.C.H.'s appearance not as distinctly long-headed but
as 'markedly dolichocephalic,' and then continued more prosaically:

> grey-white hair swept back from a furrowed brow, sunken
> grey eyes, a husky voice and a general expression of slight
> puzzlement which broke quickly either way into a smile or
> frown as he took in what you were saying, to which he paid
> you the compliment of always listening as if nothing else
> mattered.

A reviewer of *Interim* also facetiously suggested that some readers
might prefer to consider their wallpaper a little dingy rather
than their 'lincrusta rather subfusc'. R.C.H. wrote to his friend
and fellow novelist, Ernest Raymond, saying that 'Dr. Roget was
tiresome all morning (what idiotic synonyms that eager, fatuous
old man does suggest)', but the revealing comment is that R.C.H.
spent the morning browsing through Roget's suggestions and
often found him a treasure-house for exotic definitions. It is true
that R.C.H. enjoyed helping Margaret – a keen crossword-solver –
complete crosswords, but it was surely a risky assumption that all his
readers would similarly enjoy being confronted with such linguistic
challenges?

Another idiosyncratic narrative quirk, presumably an extension
of his pleasure in blurring the lines of reality and illusion, was his
occasional use of what may be described as 'dummy' prefaces –
sometimes elaborate acknowledgements to authentic but entirely
fictitious sources. He started with *Thou Hast A Devil* which opens
with a long letter from a friend of Guy's father who never reappears
in the novel. In *Testament* he writes a preface, signed by himself
from Birdlip, in which he explains that what follows is a virtually
unedited account of events of a manuscript, discovered in Paris,
written by the narrator of the following story. It is duly signed off
on the final page as written in Paris. On the following page he gives
the author's assurance that the characters in the preceding pages are

entirely fictitious. Similarly *Johanna at Daybreak* opens with thanks to Dutch sources for authentic evidence of events and of the character of Johanna herself (in fact invented). On the other hand, *Recollection of a Journey*, the only novel based on actual events, has no preface but simply traditional assurance of the fictitious nature of the people and many places in the book.

R.C.H.'s desire for privacy did not mean any lack of interest in the writings of his contemporaries, and he took pleasure in the appreciation of his work from such fellow writers as Compton Mackenzie, Cecil Day Lewis, Stevie Smith, J.B. Priestley, Edwin Muir, Kate O'Brien, Sean O'Faolain, Stephen Spender, Alex Comfort, Edith Walton, Walter Allen, John Betjeman, and Eddie Sackville-West. Although he often claimed letter-writing to be a duty rather than a pleasure, the evidence suggests the opposite, and his correspondence with other writers covers letters, often of mutual admiration, from L.P. Hartley, Joyce Carey, Rose Macaulay, Elizabeth Taylor, Helen Thomas, Robert Gittings, Ivy Compton-Burnett, A.P. Herbert, Storm Jameson, Vita Sackville-West, and Elizabeth Bowen. A letter from Rebecca West includes a rather eccentric and amusing admission: 'I liked *Testament* and *Elephant and Castle* to the point of suddenly speaking about them in speeches which were supposed to be on another subject – I just felt it was better for everybody, including me, that it should be so.' And in a footnote she adds: 'Twice this happened.'

An unusual literary meeting took place at Lord's Cricket Ground in 1946, when R.C.H. was a guest of Alec Waugh (brother of Evelyn) who had taken a box for the match against India. Waugh recorded the event in his autobiography *The Best Wine Last*, also mentioning that 'my Beaujolais was as much admired as my sandwiches':

> Among my guests that day was R.C. Hutchinson ... An acquaintance had developed into a friendship; he was a delightful fellow, completely without conceit in spite of his high quality as a writer. His talk that day was one of the most pleasant features of the occasion. We had a lot to tell each other about our writing plans. 'We must keep in touch with one another,' we agreed. But we were never to meet again. It was very easy to lose touch in postwar England ...
> I think he was one of the most significant writers of our day ... He had a miraculous capacity to make real a place that he had never visited.

Five closer associations were established which initiated more sustained correspondence. Hugh Walpole, in his heyday as a popular novelist during 1920s and 1930s, was renowned for his passionate enthusiasms for discovering new writers and was overwhelmed by reading *The Unforgotten Prisoner*. Having described it in *John O'London's Weekly* as 'the best novel of 1933 by a new author', he continued to champion R.C.H., writing favourable reviews of *Testament* and *The Fire and the Wood*, and corresponding with R.C.H. between 1936 and 1938. Walpole was fond of making lists of writers he felt would 'make the grade' and, though they are personal opinions, two such lists compiled in 1938 give some insight into the world of contemporary popular fiction at the time that R.C.H. was emerging as a literary presence. In January 1938, Walpole listed in *The Star* three young novelists from whom we might expect 'great things': Graham Greene, Christopher Isherwood, and R.C. Hutchinson. In December of that year he compiled for the *Daily Sketch* a list of 'a dozen leading contemporary English novelists', including R.C.H., alongside H.G. Wells, Somerset Maugham, Virginia Woolf, E.M. Forster, Aldous Huxley, J.B. Priestley, Elizabeth Bowen, Rose Macaulay, Frank Swinnerton, L.A.G. Strong, and Charles Morgan. (It should be stressed that the popular novelist A.S.M. Hutchinson, author of the best-selling novel of 1921, *If Winter Comes*, was no relation of, and had no connection with, R.C.H.).

A closer personal relationship was formed with the poet, novelist, journalist, and critic Richard Church – particularly popular for his 1955 autobiographical volume *Over the Bridge* (including some remarkable mystical reminiscences), and for his vivid writing about the Kent countryside. He was a regular book reviewer for *Country Life*. He became an admirer of R.C.H. after reading *Shining Scabbard*, for which he wrote a full introduction for the 1968 second English edition which remained one of the few overviews of R.C.H. as a novelist (one reviewer describing it as 'fulsome'). Church was particularly taken by the ending of the novel, when Séverin sends some of his family into retreat, in R.C.H.'s words: 'As if to remind them of the need for hurry the guns were in voice again, answering versicle with antiphon from north to south across the sky's wide haunches.' Church and R.C.H. corresponded regularly between 1957 and 1968 soon after their first meeting, which Church describes in the opening letter: 'It was as though we had met after long acquaintance. Perhaps we are old soldiers together on our relative battlefields of words?' *A Child Possessed* is dedicated to Church.

The novelists Ernest and Diana Raymond became close friends and correspondents. Ernest was a prolific writer, publishing 46 novels, including *Tell England* (1922) set in Gallipoli where he had served as an army chaplain. He resigned Holy Orders in 1923 but in later life returned to his previous Christian convictions. He met R.C.H. in the late 1930s (they had been fellow speakers at the Cheltenham Literary Festival in 1938). They were mutual admirers of each other's work and R.C.H. wrote an appreciative article for the *Camden Journal* in 1968 on Ernest's writing and an obituary of him for the Royal Society of Literature in 1974. In 1941, Ernest married Diana Young, his second wife, who was already an established writer with the publication of *Lily's Daughter*. Diana also struggled with orthodox views of Christianity and Anglicanism, but like Ernest became reconciled to a more conventional position in later years. She was also a prolific writer (publishing 24 novels). Thus remarkably, between the two of them, they produced 70 novels. They were regular visitors to R.C.H. and Margaret as well as correspondents, and they became joint dedicatees of *Johanna at Daybreak*.

The most extensive correspondence was that with the poet Martyn Skinner. Now an almost forgotten literary figure, Skinner achieved some success in the 1940s, winning the Hawthornden prize for his lengthy narrative poem *Letters to Malaya*, followed by the publication of two further narrative poems, *The Return of Arthur* and *Old Rectory*. Skinner and R.C.H. first met in 1939, in Birdlip, where Skinner's mother-in-law had a cottage. Their friendship developed after the war, as did their respect for each other's writings, and a correspondence of some 150 lengthy letters crossed between them mostly during the years 1957 and 1974. A selection of them was published as *Two Men of Letters*, edited by Rupert Hart-Davis in 1979.

It is clear, then, that when R.C.H. was at his desk reading, or researching and writing his novels, he was also spending considerable time in correspondence. Jeremy Hutchinson remembers asking at his father's funeral how many of the few hundred in the assembled company had received a letter from R.C.H. in recent years: at least half of those present raised a hand.

The correspondence with Martyn Skinner reveals much about R.C.H.'s thoughts on the intricacies of the novelist's art. In particular he talks freely about challenges of characterisation. In a lengthy passage he observes:

> You raise topics which a creature of my incurable verbosity had best not embark on. On the creation of character in fiction, however, you are safe, because that is one of the few aspects of the trade on which I cannot talk till the cows come home. I just don't know how one sets about it. The process, I should say, is quasi-mathematical: 'For my purpose, x must be the sort of man who pleases y and infuriates z, y collects postage stamps, z detests sentimentality, therefore etc.' But an instance may have some bearing on this odd business. I once required, to play a small part in a novel, a German pathologist. It seemed to me, as I joggled this puppet, that he was a lively one – I felt that it was he rather than I who moved the strings. Much later – after the publication of the book – I realised that I had drawn a tolerably faithful portrait of the chief clerk of an office I worked in at Norwich. I am inclined to think that perhaps the greater part in the creation of character is played by the *reader*. The writer gives a hint or two, and the reader unconsciously thinks, 'Ah, yes, the type of my idiotic uncle Paul,' and does the rest for himself. Yes, I do believe that a novelist's work is richer (and should come more easily) if he spends a lot of time with other people of every kind. But – the problem is permanent and almost universal – how in one lifetime both to live and to work? (especially if one has a 1 m.p.h. mind like mine). So one goes on drawing (I suppose) from old wells. I had eight years in business, five and a half in the army, besides school and Oxford. The army, especially, provided rich fare in individuals and types (none of which I've ever consciously used). At present all I learn about the human race (again, nothing I seem able to use) comes from my daughters, one a welfare officer in the Church of England's Children's Society, the other a Probation Officer in a North London court. The people *they* meet would fill a hundred novels by Dickens or Zola. I listen to them entranced – especially to the younger (just married), who happens to be a quite brilliant talker, infinite in compassion but with a devastating wit.

In his article for *The Listener* in 1953 entitled 'My First Novel', R.C.H. makes further revealing observations about the novelist's relationship with his characters – and goes a significant step further than considering characterisation as simply a matter of portraying a personality, seeing it rather as a pivotal interaction between external and internal observation:

> The really shocking thing about my first book was that it was 'manufactured'. It contained an idea which was genuine – something I felt about intensely – but instead of letting that idea grow into a book I built a ramshackle edifice with just one room to house it. Nothing resembling a work of art can be produced like that. And yet I do believe, now, that the impulse which made me set to work and churn out those 80,000 words was not merely a puerile wish to startle and impress my friends. Something else, I think, was at work, something I can only explain like this: Suppose you are in Paris, travelling on the Metro. Standing near you there is a very old and very dirty woman, wearing those unbelievably thick, black stockings which are almost the uniform of her kind. Beside her there is a tiny, white-faced boy with spindle legs and a dribbly nose. The train lurches violently, and the old woman puts her hand on the boy's shoulder to steady him. He looks up at her, perhaps with a slight impatience, because he thinks he is too old for that sort of mothering. She looks down at him, and smiles faintly. Then he smiles back. You know, at once, that he is her grandson – possibly her only grandchild. You know, at the same moment, that all her love, all her pride, are centred in him. But much more than that. In the instant when those two people exchange smiles you see represented a huge tract of human experience – you feel, all at once, that in the excitement and the beauty of that exchange, every-thing in earth and Heaven has been revealed to you. That is a common experience; I suppose nearly everyone has had something like it. And most people – being sensible – are content to preserve it as a memory. But there is a kind of person so afflicted, mentally, that he cannot be happy until he has tried to get the experience into a form in which it can be imparted to someone else. The whole of it, I mean.

Not just the incident, but the significance of it – the entire
world of relationships and feelings which the incident has
called into the light. And this kind of person is compelled
to make that attempt, even if it cost him five years' hard
labour and half a million words.

This vivid description of R.C.H.'s search for an authentic authorial
voice may well be what Richard Church was suggesting when he
claimed that 'one *lives* rather than reads his books'. And R.C.H.'s
suggestion of the 'hard labour' of producing 'half a million words'
certainly shows that he shared T.S. Eliot's famous assertion that:

Words strain,
Crack and sometimes break, under the burden,
Under the tension, slip, slide, perish,
Decay with imprecision, will not stay in place,
Will not stay still…

In a later paragraph of 'My First Novel', R.C.H. concludes:

words are a recalcitrant metal to work in. – they resist
you, the patterns they fall into are stale patterns, they
obliterate subtleties, they can kill the ideas you mean
them to illuminate… And the man who has the writer's
disease will never accept the truth that the possibilities
of language are limited. He knows well enough that book
after book has failed to convey the magic of life as he
has seen it. But he still believes that in the next one – or
the one after that – he will capture that mystery, he will
achieve the impossible, he will produce something which
perfectly satisfies himself.

It is clear that the desire to find the precision that a writer searches
for in terms of vocabulary is evident in R.C.H.'s constant perusal
of Roget's *Thesaurus*, but it is also evident in his concerns to find
the appropriate structure in his plotting, for (particularly after the
war) his novels increasingly go through several revisions before
reaching their published version. These revisions can show intriguing
developments in the process of composition, especially in the case of
his unfinished final novel *Rising*. The surviving manuscripts of *Image*

of My Father can serve as an example of a novel which took nearly four years to reach completion:

1. 33 pages of early notes
2. 390 further pages of working notes
3. 765 pages of a completed rough draft
4. 582 pages of a later draft
5. 49 pages of a revision of the closing chapter
6. 41 pages of a later version of the closing chapter
7. 640 pages of a final typescript, including further revisions

Certainly in later years he found writing to be an increasingly slow process as he became more self-critical, often starting the day by deleting almost everything he had written the day before. In 1959, he complained to Martyn Skinner that:

> I am all ready to write six plays next week; a travel book or two; and then another novel in five hundred thousand words. But meanwhile the business of sitting at a desk, opening a drawer, forcing my eyes to *look* at the loathsome maze of insertions and deletions which represents yesterday's work, is, morning after morning, evening after evening, an effort like that of climbing onto the scaffold.

It was not just some kind of inertia that was troubling him. There was a deeper and more significant personal artistic frustration that was at work. He explored the problem at some length in a further article for *The Listener* in 1953, entitled 'The Pace for Living'. The telling word is 'for' rather than the expected 'of'. He felt strongly that there was a deep-rooted change in society that was reflected in the concept of speed as a sign of how the human psyche interpreted the fundamental experience of living. He had no quarrel with the actual physical sensation of fast movement – he admitted to the pleasure of fast driving and the sense of speed when flying. But there was a more symbolic sense of the increasing speed of everyday life blurring the powers of sympathetic understanding of the undercurrents that lie beneath the surface of human feelings (often of suffering) which can only be fully sensed by unrushed interaction and observation. It is probably why train journeys (often longer, slower journeys or their imminence) are so often the chosen stage for moments of emotional exposure in his novels. It is no surprise that his suggested portrayal of the revealing smiles between grandmother and grandson take place on the Paris Metro.

He suggests that both the cinema and the theatre have reflected this change of pace, and just as he had suggested that the *reader* is a vital partner in the novelist's ability to create convincing characterisation, the *audience's* expectations have dictated the film director's and dramatist's sense of appropriate structure and pace of presentation.

The final section of the article illustrates these ideas most acutely, and because they might indeed be a key factor in explaining R.C.H.'s change in fortune in terms of popular readership, they deserve to be quoted at some length:

> And surely it would be surprising if people who have grown accustomed to a much faster movement in films and plays were content with written fiction which went at the old speeds. Of course they are not. Editors, who presumably know what their customers want, are demanding shorter and shorter stories with faster and faster action – stories which go off the mark like Olympic sprinters and keep up the pace right through to the tape. In America, where they carry these things to a logical conclusion, they have developed a technique for teaching people to read more quickly, and at the same time they have introduced devices for giving them less to read. They have literary surgeons over there who can take a novel of well over 400 pages, and with a skill that really is astonishing, they can strip it down to forty pages – using the author's own sentences, or parts of them, giving you most of the plot and nearly all the characters; and even a dash or two of the original scenery.
>
> Before long they may be able to turn out a pre-digested version of Dante's *Divina Commedia* which the tired business man can assimilate in fifteen minutes by stop-watch.
>
> I confess I do not like this. I have a professional interest in fiction – I am a producer of that class of merchandise – and I believe that the novel, as distinct from the short story or novelette, is meant to be a slow form of art. It would be presumptuous for an author to dogmatize about what the novelist's business is: that can be left to the younger critics.

But it is fairly safe to say that one of the most interesting things (I avoid the word 'important') that novelists have done in the past is the creation of characters so immense in stature and significance that they have become part of the civilised world's inheritance; and as a rule these tremendous figures of fiction have been created by a slow process. The writers have asked for a large amount of the reader's time, sometimes a good deal of his patience; and by using a very great number of small, skilful strokes, they have gradually, slowly, brought the whole man to life.

As I see it, the stature and slowness go together. It can be argued that Tolstoy, for example, was a wickedly discursive writer, that he was guilty of all sorts of irrelevance. But I wonder if Anna Karenina would be what she is to us – at once a woman of colossal tragic stature and an intimate acquaintance – if Tolstoy had squeezed her portrait into the length of *The Vicar of Wakefield*. Again, could Don Quixote, the romantic half-wit, have become a person who seems in some way to represent the aspirations and the weakness of all humanity, if Cervantes had confined his adventures so that they could be read in a couple of hours? It is said very often that the writers of our own day are incapable of creating important characters. That may be true. But if they were to ask for the patience which their predecessors confidently expected, would they get it, from readers who are used to the accelerated action of the films, people who have to do all their reading between Woking and Waterloo stations, because travel has become so rapid and convenient that there is no time to read in a chair at home?

I can see that on the face of it my objection is rather ridiculous. I seem to be saying, in effect, that there is something 'wrong' about the tempo of our own day because it does not suit the convenience of one or two old-fashioned literary types who hanker after a particular kind of writing. Of course, the complaint is not worth a moment's attention – unless the sort of writing I have mentioned does in fact correspond with something permanent in human experience; unless the slownesses in life itself which such writing reflects are something of unalterable value.

But I believe there are such slownesses. The rhythms of nature remain unchanged, and in that sense the tempo at which we live is not affected by the tempo at which we tear about. To live to the age of seventy takes seventy years. You cannot get there any faster; and at that age I doubt if your wealth – by which I mean the richness of your collected experience – will depend much on how many impressions you have been able to gather in quick succession. I am not saying that those impressions are worthless. But it seems likely that when they follow each other very rapidly each of them will cut a little less deep than the one before. And surely the most valuable part of one's mental baggage will always be made up of things which have taken time to happen: one's journey through the school years; the making of a garden; the growth of one's children. Those friendships which open and close in one season, however delightful, count for less, I think, than those which go on intermittently through the years. Love, in its largest meaning, is a thing of protracted growth, always revealing new depths, new kinds of understanding; and the satisfaction we get from lesser relationships – from our service to a firm or profession, for example – seems to be built up from a long series of adjustments, infinitely gradual changes.

You will agree, surely, that these slow and subtle processes are at least an ingredient in the happiness that is possible to human beings; and it is not hard to see that they can only be appreciated slowly. But, going a little further, I suggest that because we are creatures of very slow growth – because until the day of our death we perhaps never reach maturity – it is important for us to be aware of those slow processes while they are occurring. Is it not possible that what they call 'the nervous strain of modern life' comes partly from the disconnection between the pace at which we receive impressions and the far slower pace at which we are able to absorb experience? Are our minds being geared to a speed which blurs reality? Are we missing the scenery – losing something which is essential to our contentment and perhaps to our human dignity?

For myself, I cannot get away from the idea that the older kind of literature, the kind that explores life as a connoisseur would, taking its time, might still be of use in bridging that gap. To study lives patiently, as that sort of literature does, might show us certain harmonies in our own which we have not had time to realise. But that is merely a hobby-horse of my own. It may well be that we have finally outgrown that sort of writing. And perhaps the deep satisfactions it represented, the poetry of quietness and slow accomplishment, are something we have outgrown as well.

In these revealing paragraphs R.C.H. may well be writing his own epitaph, reflecting his dwindling readership, as he ruefully sees himself joining the band of 'old-fashioned literary types'. His most fruitful year in terms of literary income was 1959 (c.£4,000; c.£80,000 in 2020 figures), thereafter he rarely reached more than half that figure. Yet, both *Johanna at Daybreak* and *A Child Possessed* were published after 1959 – two novels in which many readers would share Rupert Hart-Davis's opinion that R.C.H. was reaching the 'apogee' of his literary skill. Perhaps, some 50 years later, there is an audience more receptive to the writing of 'quietness and slow accomplishment', more ready to 'explore life as a connoisseur would', to 'study lives patiently' and to 'show us certain harmonies in our lives which we had not time to realise'. This combination of form and content, illuminating the portrayal of the 'entire world of relationships and feelings' which can lie beneath an exchange of smiles, is in essence the true voice of R.C.H. as a novelist. This gift was succinctly captured by an anonymous writer in *The Times Literary Supplement* in 1969:

> Mr. Hutchinson's fictions stretch away behind him through three decades, spaced out like massive and stately mansions along some private avenue where nobody walks but he. They are spacious, constructed by a dedicated craftsman quick to reject anything shoddy or faked, and are all immediately recognizable as the work of the same hand.

And to where do these 'avenues' lead? The major themes seem universal enough – the consequences of war on survivors, the impact of physical and mental stress that affect human behaviour (often as a result of conflict), and the power of religion to influence human hopes and fears. These elements are not hermetically sealed in individual novels, but, as we shall see, spread themselves with varied emphasis from volume to volume as they become more and more central to R.C.H.'s narrative vision. As so often, the seeds of this imaginative quest are revealed in his schoolboy diary. He recalls a visit to Bath Abbey with his aunt and records:

> What interests me most are the little stones, tucked away behind the big ones; very few people seem to notice them. 'Here lies Mary Smith. Born 1716. Died 1773'. What was Mary Smith like, I wonder. Possibly the Abbey charters would have something about her.

Even as a teenager, he was interested in ordinary people, later bringing them to the foreground as they often become the chess-pieces of tyrannous powers. And in the final line of this diary entry, he seems to know that he will be filling his hours digging for information in the equivalent of the Abbey charters.

R.C.H. was fond of quoting Voltaire on the lonely, introverted world of the writer, and in a paragraph in 'My First Novel', he uses this as a starting point for a description of how, perhaps, he would like to see himself at his desk, in a variety of studies, his fountain pen in his hand:

> Voltaire, I think it was, said that if he had a son who wanted to write, he would strangle him out of sheer loving kindness. I recognise the wisdom of that remark. Of the ways of making a living which I have tried, writing is very much the hardest, as well as the loneliest. There must be few occupations quite so rich in disappointments. But, if you have the novelist's bacillus inside you, you will never be really contented, I think, in any other trade.

R.C.H.'s most regular correspondents.

Richard Church.

Ernest Raymond.

Diana Raymond.

Sir Hugh Walpole.

Martyn Skinner.

R.C.H., with pipe.

Chapter 5

R.C.H. and War

Of R.C.H.'s seventeen published novels, nine are specifically centred on warfare and revolution, and another five have secondary or passing references to military activity. But (R.C.H. being idiosyncratic as ever) none of them fits into what might be considered typical accounts based on survivors' memories.

Most British readers in the 1940s interested in the literary accounts of the First World War would be familiar with the wealth of poetry written during the war – particularly from writers such as Siegfried Sassoon, Edmund Blunden, Ivor Gurney, David Jones, Isaac Rosenberg, Edward Thomas, and from the familiar words of Rupert Brooke (though commissioned and written in the very early months of the war) and the extraordinarily prophetic words of Laurence Binyon ('Age shall not wither them…') heard each Remembrance Day, but in fact written as early as 1914. Most of all, they would have been familiar with the voice of Wilfred Owen, killed in Arras in 1918.

In prose, the emphasis was on personal memoirs represented predominantly by Siegfried Sassoon, Edmund Blunden, and Robert Graves. Less common were reminiscences through novels, with the exception of such works as R.H. Mottram's *The Spanish Farm Trilogy*.

The literature of the Second World War moved in a quite different direction for a variety of reasons (one being that warfare became increasingly involved in the battlefields of the air, rather than endless hours suffered by many young, educated infantrymen in the First World War's trenches, which offered little diversion than that offered by pen and notebook). Coming from a quite different background,

Ivor Gurney was able to write music in his notebook with the stub of a pencil.

Poetry in the Second World War was remembered mostly through the works of three young writers, Keith Douglas, Alun Lewis, and Sidney Keyes, all of whom died in military service, Lewis being the oldest casualty at age 28.

The world of prose also took a different direction – novels becoming more popular than reminiscences (with exceptions, notably Keith Douglas's *Alamein to Zem Zem*) but they tended to be novels from already established authors, such as Evelyn Waugh, Henry Green, Patrick Hamilton, Elizabeth Bowen, and H.E. Bates (who was commissioned into the Royal Air Force solely to write inspiring short stories, before being posted to the Far East). There were, of course, some new writers who came to prominence as novelists – notably Alexander Baron, whose *From the City, From the Plough*, became heralded as England's version of Remarque's *All Quiet on the Western Front*.

As we have seen, R.C.H. was not a poet and his novels dealing with the First World War (*The Unforgotten Prisoner* and *Shining Scabbard*) cover events in post-war Germany and the prelude to the Prussian invasion of France at a time when R.C.H. was not yet a teenager. *Testament* (for many the core novel in the Hutchinson oeuvre) depicting the Bolshevik rebellion was also written about historical moments which took place at a time when R.C.H. was still a child. It is thus particularly interesting to review R.C.H.'s own experience between 1939 and 1945.

In 1939, he had joined the Officers' Emergency Reserve, becoming an infantry officer training new recruits (after minimal training himself) in the wilds of Devon and Cornwall. In March 1939, he was commissioned to serve with 'The Buffs' (the Royal East Kent Regiment), travelling the country training the Home Guard – the local defence force formerly known as the Local Defence Volunteers which ran from 1940 to 1944 and consisted of those who, from ages 17 to 65, were either too young, too old, or were unfit to serve, or were otherwise ineligible.

Three years later, he joined the Staff College in Camberley, and in 1943 he was transferred to the War Office in London to work for the Directorate of the Home Guard. To enable this last transfer he lived in a top-floor bedsit in Kensington during the week, and his Home Guard experiences provided the inspiration for the only novel written during the war itself, *Interim* (mostly penned in the evenings in his London room, with the constant sound of bombing as his companion). It is an unusual work, even by R.C.H.'s standards, being his shortest (almost a novella) and being one of only two novels set entirely in England (the other being *Elephant and Castle*, intriguingly his second longest). When asked why he so seldom set his novels in England, he liked to say that it was because the English offered less interest for him as a nation, but this was almost certainly said with his tongue in his cheek – more likely he felt happier when stretching his imagination to meet the greater narrative demands and challenges presented by depicting events set in places unknown to him.

Interim is a novel with a minimum of action. An assorted number of servicemen find themselves brought together at various times in a house named Orchilly in the British West Country, the home of a doctor, ex-missionary in China, and Anglican lay reader named Quindle, who holds open house to soldiers on leave. The novel is narrated by a soldier, Roger, who is waiting for transfer to Africa. The figure of Quindle is based on an acquaintance of R.C.H.'s, the Reverend T.W. Griffiths, rector of St Bride's, Pembrokeshire, who gave hospitality to many servicemen.

Apart from the fact that the setting is wartime Britain and that the book ends with the military story of the wartime experience of Quindle's son, Bernard, the novel might not be classed as war fiction at all. It is aptly entitled *Interim* for it deals with interruptions and suspensions of feelings and certainties in the lives of the characters – and perhaps also in the life of its author. It is a work which very much achieves its impact through evocations of atmosphere. Roger feels a magnetic attraction to a sense of possible personal fulfilment that Orchilly seems to offer. The reader comes to know every room in the house – the furniture and proportions of each are presented in detail. We get to know the sounds of the kitchen, the smell of the pet dogs, and the slightly threatening world inhabited by Quindle's invalid wife. (R.C.H.'s skill in painting vivid impressions of interiors will be developed further in *The Stepmother*.) Roger's infatuation with the house – which was a place he originally broke into but then found difficult to leave – moves towards some sort of psychological self-analysis, which is closely associated with his developing friendship (almost hero-worship) with Quindle, his affection for Quindle's daughter, Virginia, and an increasing understanding with the lonely figure of Quindle's wife, Charlotte.

War, medicine, and religion are all intimately intertwined. R.C.H.'s friend Derek Severn in a BBC Radio Three broadcast in September 1976, 'R.C. Hutchinson: A Neglected Genius', acutely described *Interim* as a 'search of lonely and dislocated characters for spiritual wholeness – in effect for Resurrection'. Not everyone shared this enthusiasm. Reviews, as usual, varied between extremes of praise and critical dismissal. Philip Toynbee, writing in the *New Statesman*, dipped his pen into especially vitriolic ink, describing the novel as 'positively and virulently vulgar' and, in its 'official opposition' to modern materialism, a 'melange of platitude ... shallow ... kitsch'. On the other hand, Richard Church found the novel one of R.C.H.'s best works, almost Conradian, and 'desperately moving'. Walter Allen found it 'intolerably facetious' and 'vulgar'. Howard Spring thought it 'short but perfect' and confirmed Hutchinson's place as 'one of the few significant novelists of our day'.

One problem for the contemporary reader is the constant use of the euphemism 'fumin' in the soldier's conversation. Perhaps a reissue with this restriction removed could bring fresh life to the dialogue for new readers.

R.C.H.'s work at the War Office provided a remarkable and unexpected unique literary challenge. On 3 December 1944, there was an official stand-down parade of the Home Guard in Hyde Park and King George VI was to make an official speech as a tribute. R.C.H. was asked to write the King's speech, which he was both honoured and amused to do. The King's broadcast on the declaration of war on Germany was brought to wide public attention in 2011 by the film 'The King's Speech', cleverly combining the content of the speech with the debilitating speech impediment of the King's sometimes uncontrollable stammer. The Home Guard speech was another rare occasion on which the King braved the radio airwaves for an extended broadcast. The authorship of the speech was supposed to remain anonymous but R.C.H.'s pen was somehow revealed the next day in the national press – it was applauded for its ability to capture the King's tones and speech patterns as though the King had written it himself (only one sentence was altered from the original script). R.C.H. wrote to Ernest Raymond explaining that he tried to capture 'the unique combination of informality and moderate pomposity appropriate to the occasion'. Even R.C.H.'s patience was exercised as he listened to the broadcast with his younger daughter, Elspeth, who remembered him muttering to the wireless set: 'Oh, for goodness sake, get it out man!'

One wonders whether R.C.H. remembered what he had written to Margaret in a letter in the 1920s before their marriage: 'At the age of about six I declared three ambitions: to marry the most wonderful woman in the world, to fly an aeroplane and to shake hands with the King.' After the writing of the King's speech, perhaps he may have felt that, in his mind, although not shaking hands with the monarch, he had achieved his early hopes!

In 1945, events changed dramatically for R.C.H. 'The Buffs' had sent troops to the Middle East who were to become part of what was to become known as 'The Third Army'. R.C.H. was sent to Baghdad for four months to write the history of the campaign in Persia and Iraq (known by the acronym Paiforce).

To many in 1941, it must have seemed strange that the field of warfare had extended to the relatively unknown territories of Persia and Iraq, and their surrounding countries. These were lands which probably evoked thoughts of rich trading posts, exotic art and architecture, and a history of political violence over many centuries, but few could claim much detailed knowledge. The great rivers of the Tigris and the Euphrates and the romantic sound of Mesopotamia were familiar names, but could they be confidently placed in an atlas? Some would have learnt at Sunday school of Darius, Cyrus, and Nebuchadnezzar and knew the story of Shadrach, Meshach, and Abednego surviving death by fire – but it remained just that: a stirring story. Secondary school may have introduced them, via Byron, to the Assyrian assault on Sennacherib – but they were poetic names rather than historical ones. Marlowe's violent dramas on Tamburlaine were exciting reading, but they took place in worlds as real as C.S. Lewis's Narnia or J.R.R. Tolkien's Middle Earth. So why were the eyes of the Allies and Germany now concentrated on this geographical arena, a mixture of extremes of intense cold and suffocating heat, limited internal communications, and certainly not a natural battlefield? The answer lay in one three-letter word, much more familiar to later generations as of huge political and economic significance: oil. In 1940, in general terms, over half the world's oil lay in the USA. Of the remainder, the larger fraction lay in Russia and most of the remaining fraction lay in Persia and Iraq: thousands and thousands of gallons of it. It was thus essential to the Allied powers to have friendly relations with both countries; it was equally essential to Germany to prevent or subvert such collaboration. (Access to natural resources contributed to conflict elsewhere at this time; for example, Malaya – under British control until 1941-2, when the Japanese invaded – was home to supplies of rubber and tin).

But it was not just oil that was at stake – altogether some 5 million tons of a variety of materials were transported across desert and mountain, by water, road and rail, from the Gulf to Russia. It was thus a logistical rather than a purely military campaign, which particularly intrigued R.C.H.'s imagination. He undertook considerable travelling himself, recording his first official meeting with a Russian: 'She was a Soviet Army sergeant who pulled a pistol on me as I drove along a Persian mountain road which was frequented by Russian convoys. Fortunately my papers were in order.'

Paiforce needed to be written at some speed and, as he was constantly aware, R.C.H. was becoming an increasingly slow worker: 'I have an abnormally *slow* mind, and this means I take far longer to write a page of prose than most people.' But his fascination with the combination of the extraordinary mixture of technical knowledge and bravery, in what he described as a good epitaph for the campaign ('Paiforce enabled five million tons of provisions to go to Russia'), seemed to spur his pen to greater speed.

The tone of the account is distinctly different from most military records. In what is in effect a short work of some 140 pages, it covers the historical background to the creation of Persia and Iraq as the highway to the British Raj in India, the British presence between 1919 and 1933, the confusing tensions between the Shias and Sunnis and other nomadic tribes, and the German influence both politically and economically between 1933 and 1941, before the Germans invaded Greece and established a strategic air-base in Crete. He records vividly the extraordinary defence of the airport in Habbaniya and then concentrates on the massive effort of conveying supplies to Russia. (What strange echoes must have come to him from his imaginative explorations in the tundra described in *One Light Burning*?)

It is clear that R.C.H. could not divorce himself from having the novelist's eye as well as the eye of the objective historian. The most perceptive review of *Paiforce* came from the pen of Robert Green, a life-long admirer of R.C.H. and compiler of a magnificent working bibliography of R.C.H. published in 1985. He contributed an essay to *The Army Quarterly and Defence Journal* in 1985, 'Paiforce: The Novelist as Military Historian'. The novelist's perspective is evident

on the first page of *Paiforce* as R.C.H. describes a meeting of old
soldiers in a drill-hall in 1941 (an entirely imaginary occasion) after
the news that the Allies had landed in Iraq:

> Iraq? Was it something to do with the Air Force? But men
> with moustaches turning grey, who talked in a corner of
> a drill-hall before the evening Home Guard parade, knew
> something about Iraq. 'Mespot' they said. So that was
> starting again! Heat like the opening of an oven door, the
> flies, the pack-mules, the mihailas; heat-stroke, dysentery:
> time had blurred the details, but they remembered
> Mesopotamia as a kind of delirium, a brown and yellow
> nightmare. And now another crowd, sons of their own
> perhaps, were to go through that.

Paiforce was eventually published – after official bureaucratic
delays – in 1948. It was published anonymously under the auspices
of His Majesty's Stationery Office, but R.C.H.'s authorship quickly
became known. The reviewer in the *Yorkshire Evening Post* criticised
the volume because it 'does not get below the level of the brass hats and
brigadiers in assessing all that happened' and lacks 'human interest'.
It transpired that the reviewer was responsible for persuading the
relevant authorities that such an account should be written and perhaps
he felt that he could have done a better job. One wonders though if he
had read the whole account. It is true that R.C.H. made several close
contacts with the 'top brass' both military and civilian – he became
particularly friendly with Sir Reader William Bullard who became
Ambassador to Iran and with whom he corresponded until 1974. But
had the reviewer read the description of the Syrian excursion:

> Behind the strange and daring campaign in Syria there is
> a complex picture of men's activity spread over a thousand
> miles: a harassed Yorkshireman hunting for tools in
> the bazaars of Basra; men from Ambala and Siddipett
> performing, in the milky light of a hurricane lamp, surgery
> on the buckled chassis of a Studebaker; patched lorries
> bumping over sleepers on the Samawa railway bridge;
> a boy from Sukkur who fights to keep awake as his ten-
> ton Mack Diesel heaves and rattles along the sand-swept
> Haditha road. On these many human strands, stretched to

the limit, the success of the campaign depended. They did not break.

In March 1946, R.C.H. wrote a long letter to *The Times* clearly defining his aim in writing *Paiforce*. He praised the Royal Engineers for the huge constructional programme of developing the Trans-Iranian railway, despite chaotic, Gilbertian official lack of organization:

> Working double-headed trains through the 140 tunnels (some spiral) between Andimeshk and Dorud, British locomotive crews were often overcome by fumes and the terrible heat. Some Sappers died; but the loads that the Russians so desperately needed always got through. By the end of 1942 the monthly lift had been multiplied nearly eight times ... The whole story had to be kept dark for reasons of security, and in consequence a splendid achievement by thousands of British and Indian soldiers in the conquest of distance and climate has received pitifully small recognition.

Many readers would feel that *Paiforce* redresses that balance. In particular, any suggestion that R.C.H. paid little attention to the ordinary soldier and that the volume lacks human interest can be quickly dismissed by quoting R.C.H.'s final paragraph, even if the somewhat jingoistic tone may jar on the ears of some present day readers:

> Paiforce was not hand-picked and it did not consist of a team of archangels. There were tares among the wheat. But if there was also virtue, as the brief sketch of Paiforce activities in this book may have suggested, it was surely virtue of no trumpery kind. Among all the races and types which made-up the war-time population of Persia and Iraq, there is one figure which stands a little apart: not in hostility or shyness, by no means from lack of friendship, but from a certain quality that makes him older than the rest, whatever his actual age may be. He is nothing out of the ordinary, as he himself will tell you with sincerity; It is just by chance that he has a flair for learning new techniques and getting over difficulties. There he stands, near the entrance to the marshalling yards at Khanaqin, calling up

the lorries with a jerk of his thumb: his shirt and shorts limp with sweat, his topee pushed back, his arms grubby from a casual job on a Persian driver's engine; unvarying in humour and fabulous in patience; untiring, incorruptible, and in the end, invincible: the British soldier.

A remarkably vivid description of R.C.H. as a soldier comes from a letter written to Margaret after R.C.H.'s death, from the novelist (author of *Staying On* and *The Raj Quartet*) Paul Scott. One might imagine that it would be a letter from one writer about a fellow writer (and Scott was an admirer of R.C.H.'s work) but it is a rare surviving written account of R.C.H. as a personality rather than an analysis of him as a writer:

The reason I write to you is to say that quite apart from my admiration of R.C. Hutchinson as a writer I remember him as an officer in the 8 Buffs, B Company ... I was a newly joined recruit in D Company, but I had friends in Captain Hutchinson's Company and I can tell you that these young men ... thought themselves lucky to have *him* for a Company Commander, and not the others, and that one or two of these friends who were transferred to D Company deeply regretted it. The reason was of course that Capt. Hutchinson was a good man. I saw him quite often (but never spoke to him) and was much impressed to be looking at and in the presence of a man who had already done what I hoped to do one day myself – write novels. Years and years later he was good enough to come to a talk I was giving and I told him the circumstances in which we had 'met' before. We had a good laugh. But the thing is, he was much *honoured* by the young soldiers he had charge of ... I gather he thought his military career rather unsuccessful – but it wasn't, so far as young recruits were concerned ... he was the man in *that* Battalion I never heard a bad word against, and I wish he had been in command of *me* ... I didn't tell him that, when we met officially at the Royal Society of Literature, but it's what I feel ... I thought I'd drop you a line just to record this indelible memory of him – with his stick, his mittens (winter), a moustache (surely), and a smile and a look in the eye that reminded us we were all still human beings.

It is clear that although the themes of war were to remain constantly in his mind, the war itself had some negative effects on his creative success. He became acutely aware that the demands of producing work at the speed that publishers required was at odds with the speed at which his mind worked and with the speed with which he wished his readers to share his explorations of his characters' motives and hopes and fears. The unique avenues which we have seen he wished to explore, what Ivor Brown (who considered R.C.H. a 'major novelist' and 'a writer of genuine technical mastery') described in 1949 as 'Hutchinson's penetrative eye which drives into the odd corners of the soul', was beginning to lose resonance with an audience which demanded immediacy of action rather than what Alex Comfort described as R.C.H.'s 'reverie-technique', and which was becoming out of tune with contemporary taste. R.C.H. thought that the effects of war were partly responsible for this change of sympathy. Quoted in *The Leader* in 1945, R.C.H. observed:

> Like everyone else, what I require now, in order to get on with the job, is a period completely free of other preoccupations. Excellent writing can be done by men who balance typewriters on their knees in wet and windswept ditches, with other men jostling by, with the air shaken by artillery and torn with M.G. fire; or in the corners of crowded canteens with the wireless going, or on troopships, or in aircraft: men like Alan Moorehead are constantly performing this miracle. But normally *fiction* cannot be written in these conditions, and I believe that the simple reason why major fiction is hardly being written at all now is that the roar is too great and too continuous... There is no quietness, no mental quietness, in which to think.

The novel that he was working on when war broke out was *The Fire and the Wood*, which he began in 1938. It is an example like many of R.C.H.'s 'war' novels of being a novel as much about themes which are *not* about war as those that are – indeed a central issue in this case belonging more appropriately in a later chapter on medicine. But its setting is a favourite one for R.C.H., a country either recovering from or waiting for the impact of warfare. On this occasion, the setting is Germany in 1933 (when R.C.H. was 26 and written when he was 31, and had never visited Germany). Dr Josef Zeppichmann, son of a Jewish shopkeeper, is convinced that he has discovered a cure for tuberculosis and is determined to continue his research with treatments on terminal patients and by extending his experiments in medical laboratories. He is frustrated at every turn, partly by what he sees as the academic blindness of his superiors and then by the obvious distance and antipathy surrounding his Jewishness, which eventually sees him denounced to the local political activists as a dangerous communist leader and sent to a concentration camp, where the brutal regime makes for some disturbing reading. The ever-present sinister spectre of violence and brutality mixed with fervent nationalism is sharply captured in the description of Josef's imminent interrogation by Erich Meisel in the humid, draughty interior of the Victoria Club:

> [Meisel] felt a certain resentment as he followed the guard, shivering slightly along the corridor. He had understood that he belonged to an inner circle of the party, that the greatest service he could give was in the department of ideological organization. Examining prisoners was a job for the rank and file; and as to this Zeppichmann, his single wish was never to see the stinking clod again. At the foot of the staircase Rutsatz stopped. 'I've something here,' he said, 'that you might find useful. We find it saves a good deal of time in these examinations.' It was a piece of rubber pipe some three feet long. Erich said 'Thank you' and put it in his pocket. So that was the method! For just an instant, as they turned into the lower passage, he felt curiously faint; and then, with a sudden spiritual enlightenment, his courage returned. He realized now that the time had come for his vengeance, avenging not the wrongs done to himself but the insult to his blood. The fellowship in which he had sealed his life, which had claimed the whole of his young and fierce devotion, was divinely charged with a mission to cleanse and purify his land. The task that lay before him was not the pricking of a single dirty clot; it was, in symbol, an assault on the whole of the land's impurity: and in this sacred act he fought not as himself alone but as the archon

of a nation, a Parsifal in whom a people's holiness had been reborn. He touched the coil in his pocket and it seemed to have become the hilt of a sword. With a cold fire kindled in his loins and temples he forgot the smallness of his frame, the puny thighs and narrow chest, the way he must tilt his head to talk to other men. In this transfiguration the childish part of him had dropped away, he had become a warrior to his ancient heritage.

It is while he is in the prison camp that Josef forms a friendship with a fellow inmate, the elderly and very infirm musician Dahlmeyer, who, as his life drains away, advises Josef on how to survive persecution and keep his humanity intact. He describes the memory of playing Haydn and knowing that the performance had 'reached the pinnacle of interpretation, I was certain it would never be done so perfectly again.' He evokes the memory as feeling that:

> mystery was passing through my mind and hands. It becomes part of yourself, like your arms or legs, an experience such as that. Don't you think that those are the only real values! Not what we possess, but the difference our possessions make in ourselves. Not the things people do to us, but the result of their actions in our own being.

He concludes:

> 'Listen, Zeppichmann! I want to tell you something I believe. I believe that evil can't crush out the virtue which we have in common, it can only stamp it into a smaller compass – like a kernel, you see, a tiny kernel of virtue, hard as steel and desperately powerful. You've got to hang on to that – you've got something valuable to look after and take out of this place. I mean, you've got to keep your own integrity, you've got to keep your mind very clear.' Another effort, and he was fierce now. 'Don't let them get their fingers on to that, don't let them persuade you that their own silly routine of hating and hurting is the proper business of human beings! You know it isn't, you know that yourself, you know that the spirit of man is worth infinitely more than that...'

But the novel has an interlocking sub-plot. A fellow member of the lodging house in which Josef lives is a down-trodden, powerfully courageous phthisic maid, Minna, who is considered beyond medical help. Josef sees her as the ultimate clinical challenge but she soon becomes his lover rather than his patient. Her unrelenting belief in his healing powers becomes a dominant element in the narrative of the final part of the novel as Minna gradually finds some recovery and they successfully escape to England. R.C.H. sub-titled the book 'A Love Story', suggesting that this element was as central a theme as the rise of racial aggression in Germany. We shall later suggest that medical ethics may be even more central than either love or politics.

In 1945, R.C.H. was invited by Geoffrey Lawrence (later Lord Oaksey), an old friend and admirer of R.C.H., who was the main British Judge during the Nuremberg trials and President of the Judicial group, to join him in Nuremberg. The visit left an indelible mark on R.C.H. who was for ever haunted by 'the banality of evil' which he witnessed. He had ideas for planning a novel based on these impressions though it never became more than a project in his imagination, though it may well be the inspiration for one of his most powerful novels: *Johanna at Daybreak*. Once again, we shall return to aspects of this novel in a future chapter but its origins are very much based on reflections of the effects of wartime on those affected by the Holocaust. It took four years for R.C.H. to complete, beginning in 1964. One problem was the challenge of creating a narrator, entirely seen through the eyes of a disturbed female character. The concept of the 'Unreliable Narrator', a phrase coined by Wayne C. Booth three years before R.C.H. embarked on *Johanna*, links the novel in many respects with Ford Maddox Ford's 1915 novel *The Good Soldier* (a title sarcastically suggested to his publishers who were unsatisfied with Ford's original title, *The Saddest Story*). Johanna is suffering not from military action or its memories, but from the mental trauma which the war has inflicted on a painfully tormented guilt-ridden personality. She is the survivor of a mixed marriage – she was a Christian whose husband was an eminent Jewish publisher. As so often, R.C.H. juggles with real and imaginary settings, both geographically and in authenticity of narration. His evocation of place is as vivid as ever, though he had never been to Holland – where the story is partly set – and his only visit to Germany was his brief visit to the Nuremberg trials. But so convincing was his description of place and events and his assertions in his fictitious acknowledgements that a reviewer in the *New Statesman* praised the novel on sheer technical grounds for its handling of a *true* story (also suggested by the publisher's blurb). More accurate was the *Punch* reviewer who admires his telling of a story 'faultlessly' and above all that he 'invents, invents, invents'.

One of the avenues of invention was the exploration of memory, and in a variety of ways. The reader follows Johanna's battles with her own memory as though one is listening to a patient on the psychiatrist's couch. She recalls the happy past of a loving pre-war marriage and loving parenthood. The next instalment of memory is the most painful. Is she suppressing or imagining the betrayal of her husband to the Nazis (who then perished in Dachau) and has she abandoned her children? We travel with her on her tortuous journey as she tries to face what she suspects is an awful truth of ultimate betrayal. If she cannot trust her own memory, can she trust the people she meets? Her mental journey is mirrored in her physical one. We first see her in a Dutch rescue centre for displaced refugees, distrustful of everyone around her. Does she dimly recognize any of them as characters from her past? Are they even members of her family, or are they tormentors in disguise? Every conversation is a threat, a possible ambush. She must always be on the alert, and imagines that she is constantly under surveillance; all meetings may be preludes to interrogation.

This mental disturbance is intrinsically intertwined with the position of Judaism. This is forcefully captured in an undiluted vision presented by an aged and sick-ridden 'displaced person' talking to Johanna (who still suspects that all Jews are trying to force her into some kind of confession):

> 'I am more immensely conscious of my Jewishness than I ever was before – and that has a duel consciousness. It fills me with pride and gratitude for what my forbears have given me – the power of survival, the mental independence you always find in minorities, the gift of discriminating between what's merely attractive and what is permanently beautiful. But just because I've completely realised my nature as a Jew I feel I can penetrate some distance into non-Jewish ways of looking. I've come to understand profoundly some of the gentile resentments – the uneasiness they feel about people who can never be fully assimilated ... And to look at history with intelligence one needs to start with that sort of perception.'

In another section of the novel, a powerful defence of the Jewish role in history ends with the declaration: 'We have produced in every age something greater than ourselves – a message, an oracle, insisting that righteousness is an entity independent of human kind, infinite in power, exerting a unique authority.' Mervyn Horder pinpoints this moment and goes on to declare that *Johanna* is a book that 'should find its place one day as the most assured and successful, as it is the most haunting, of all the author's post-war work'.

Like Ford Maddox Ford, R.C.H. changed his title from his early draft *No Fault of Mine* to a more hopeful title including the concept of 'daybreak', but it remains a misty daybreak. As her physical journey takes her back to Germany, so the past begins (despite its horrific possibilities) to point to a future of some sort of stability: 'one cannot finally obliterate a previous life by shutting the doors of memory and turning the key'. She finds a hesitant release from her nightmare, being able to admit that 'No one's life can be divided into past and present with a thick line ruled between the two … we're made out of our own history … our past experience and the way we've dealt with it'. She knew she 'was back on the painful course I could never finally escape from – itself my one escape from the despotism of the past; the only course which could lead to an ultimate tranquillity; the harsh, acceptable, exalting road'.

It would, however, be quite unbalanced to see novels such as *The Fire and the Wood* and *Johanna at Daybreak* as unremittingly dark throughout. R.C.H. never lost his ability to create comic episodes in the midst of the bleak landscape. The description of furniture being moved in the lodgings where Josef is living has an element of farce reminiscent of the famous scene in cinema when Laurel and Hardy attempt to move a piano (screened in 1932). Indeed R.C.H. shares the mixture of humour and underlying pathos which makes the comedy of Laurel and Hardy and Charlie Chaplin so memorable. Johanna's constant companion, a fellow resident in the Dutch refugee hostel, is the ever optimistic, elderly Debora Stahl, living on *her* past memories and looking forward to a future of returning wealth and comfort to be shared by all. In her shabby dress, 'shedding her smile as a lighthouse circulates its beams', she transforms in her imagination every grim, dilapidated room into a salon in an old mansion. There is refreshing comedy in Stahl's confusion over taxis and luggage for their travel from Holland to Astelbrucke in Germany, a journey ending in a ludicrous ascent up a steep, step-laden hill, with Debora being bounced over the precipitous steps, spread-eagled in a collapsing pram, waving triumphantly to all passers-by. Most memorable is the birthday party given in the courtyard of their new home, the shambles known as 'The Warren', organised by Johanna for one of her fellow residents. Here, chaos is transformed into genuine warmth, despite the precarious lighting effects produced by another resident, 'a magician with electricity', stumbling over lengths of dangerously exposed wiring. Here ladders collide, glasses are smashed, and the highlight is a rendition of Schubert sung by a resident, a former opera singer, performing perched on a ladder, accompanying herself with one hand on a piano dangerously half-balanced across a first-floor window where it has become stuck. In all its ludicrous setting it is as heart-warming a celebration as one could wish.

Despite some warm reviews, the novel was not an immediate commercial success. Martyn Skinner, however, wrote an engaging letter of appreciation, pretending in the opening paragraph that he had just returned from:

> a rather headlong, but most vivid and life-enhancing trip abroad – so memorable that I find it difficult not to believe that I'm still there … Yes, it certainly was a most memorable trip in every way – though not perhaps always as comfortable as I would like … However, I became involved in one or two incidents and parties, hilarious and convivial, yet somehow poignant, that I wouldn't have missed for the world. There was one in particular I shall never forget – it was a birthday party in a place called Astelbrucke.

The real core of the novel, however, remains the deeply moving presentation of the necessity of understanding and forgiveness as the only answer to the horrific consequences of the evils inherent in the Holocaust. Robert Green captured its essence:

> It is a novel of reconstruction, of the individual's rebuilding of a shattered psyche, and of the physical re-creation, the 'economic miracle,' of post-war Germany. It is a sustained fictional achievement of very high order, a towering commentary on modern European history that will one day be properly assessed as a classic of our time.

R.C.H. would have been delighted to read the reactions of the *Jewish Chronicle* which described the book as 'a powerful and beautifully written plea for our tolerance'. Less complimentary was the opinion of Julian Symonds in the *Sunday Times,* stating that the novel was 'cliché-ridden'. In retrospect R.C.H. admitted that the imposed speedy proof-reading prevented him from excluding the improbability that despite her paranoia Johanna would not recognize her own children. Hutchinsonians, however, have been more generous in their judgements and many have seen the novel as one of the very best works to emerge from his pen.

The work certainly gained the admiration of Richard Harries (Baron Harries of Pentregarth), former Bishop of Oxford. He used the novel as the subject, in July 1986, for one of his many celebrated 'Thought for the Day' broadcasts for BBC Radio Four. He also expressed his view in his volume *After the Evil: Christianity and Judaism in the Shadow of the Holocaust* that 'There is nothing sentimental about the novel, no glossing over the terrible evil that has been done. The truth has to be faced. But facing that truth does not exclude reconciliation with those who have been desperately damaged.' He concludes that *Johanna at Daybreak* is 'One of the most profound novels to come out of World War Two.'

One very influential experience from his time in Persia and Iraq remained to trouble R.C.H.'s memory. From 1939 the British Army had to deal with shiploads of distraught Polish refugees dumped on the shore of the Caspian Sea by the Russians, mostly survivors of the millions whom Stalin had deported to slave labour in the Soviet Union's system of gulags. Hundreds of thousands of these 'displaced persons' had been forced to travel long distances by rail and water, on horse-drawn cart or on foot – often in one another's arms or on one another's backs. They arrived starving, ragged, exhausted both physically and mentally; often disease-ridden, many of them children. R.C.H. had witnessed these refugees disembarking in the Gulf, described in *Paiforce*:

> The ships came without warning, at all hours of the day and night, one carrying as many as five thousand ... The civilians wore old overcoats and shapeless trousers, torn shawls and faded gabardines, boots falling to bits, nondescript wrappings of greasy flannel and tattered linen. Forty in every thousand were infested with lice. Some of the women were advanced

in pregnancy, and among the children seventy orphans from three to twelve years old. This variegated multitude, unloaded onto the wharf, spilt over on to the beach and stood there in crowded groups or stopped in the roadway and sat down in the soiled snow, where curious Persian children gathered round them. Many were silent, others voluble. Some, excited by freedom and loaded with typhus, wandered off into the town. A few lay down and died.

R.C.H. was determined to find out as much as he could about their horrific journey, which destroyed not just Polish family life, but every area of national life – farmers, foresters, teachers, police, intellectuals, and civil servants, all reduced to nameless bodies of no significance.

He found particularly rich material for his research from the publication in 1947 (with a preface by T.S. Eliot) of *The Dark Side of the Moon* by Zoe Zajdlerowa, based on first-hand accounts of Poles who had survived that journey, and seen their land and society destroyed, captured in the vivid phrase: 'Even the village hearths had grown cold.' R.C.H. had access to a bald military document giving the background to the episode, and he established his own 'Table of Events', going back to 1847, imagining how an established Polish family might have experienced such humiliating and de-humanising experiences. All this was extended by meeting a survivor of this nightmare journey when R.C.H. was in Cairo, en route to Britain.

He thus created the Kolbeck family, headed by the proud and authoritarian General Julius Kolbeck and his equally imperious mother. Julius holds the sovereignty of Poland and the sanctity of the Kolbecks in equal reverence. The history of the attacks on both these ideals and the indignities which accompanied them, together with the dignity with which they were endured, became the basis for R.C.H.'s novel, *Recollection of a Journey*.

Once again the choice of narrative stance adds parallel thematic strands. The narrator, Stephanie, is an outsider from the Polish inner circle but is intrinsically linked. She does not have pure Polish blood, but Julius' son, Victor, is father of her son, Conrad (who died in infancy, another victim of the 'Journey'), and the novel is written to the only surviving Kolbeck boy, Paul, as an extended open letter. Stephanie is initially ostracised by the Kolbeck family because she is not fully Polish and the tenuous legitimacy of her relationship with Victor. But she shares the family's suffering and thus comes to be given some acceptance. We are therefore offered two interlocking themes – the persecution of a nation and the nightmare of a young girl caught in the horrors of warfare during which she loses three of her babies and a husband – the description of Stephanie desperately trying to reach her new-born son, who has been left alone in an adjoining hut in an internment camp, barred from Stephanie's protection, makes agonisingly distressing reading. It is no surprise that many of the pivotal moments of the novel take place on trains. One journey takes place with Stephanie squeezed into the company of many old, sick, dying passengers, mothers calling out the names of their children and throwing out letters to loved ones through the windows, the smell of unwashed bodies and stagnant air permeating the claustrophobic, overcrowded carriages. But the courageous defiance of the Polish spirit resounds above the misery through the vigorous singing of 'Poland shall rise, shall rise again!'

The novel had a warm reception in the USA, published under the title *Journey with Strangers*. While this title emphasises the importance of the 'journey' within the novel – as in so many of them – it fails to emphasise the importance of 'Recollection'. Just as memory is an essential element in the experience of Johanna – and it will be so again in future novels – it is a central issue for Stephanie, and Stephanie is an intriguing development in R.C.H.'s creation of female narrators. He recorded in his working notes: 'The style must have the quality of limpidity … above all it must, in itself, represent the hallucinatory feeling of the story. It must also be feminine.' Stephanie feels both the impulse to pass on her memories and the impossibility of being able to share them accurately:

> I do not sleep very well and the task of recalling even recent happenings tires me quickly. The rumble of trains passing all day continually provokes fresh memories and then confuses them…you do not picture in advance the long unravelling of a journey … No, I doubt if we can penetrate deeply the minds of those who have come before us, however much we may know about their affairs.

Thinking of the reader of her memories: 'These scraps of reminiscence may suggest an approach to life; but only life itself which teach him whether the minimum that remains when the flame has passed is enough to justify the toil of living, its valiance and its pain.'

Ultimately the novel transcends both the internal sufferings of individuals and the sufferings of a nation to touch the sufferings of humanity itself. In many ways Johanna and Stephanie are twin sisters in torment, both reflecting the cruelty inflicted by humans on each other and the effects that such suffering has on its victims. Johanna's is a more intensely mental torture, Stephanie's a more physical one; Johanna's release is more tenuous, Stephanie's a little more assured, as she evaluates what she has learnt from her fellow travellers (particularly Victor's realisation that happiness does not depend on being in one's own country) as the final passage of the novel reveals:

> But if Victor had not been restored to me ... I do not think I should have realised fully what those fellow-travellers seemed to make plain to me: that the human claim to a portion of divinity rest safely on the capacity of men to suffer, on the genius by which they transcend their sufferings. I know, at least, that during the cramped, interminable hours when our convoy was labouring to the summit of Aveh, when we crawled in a plume of dust across the seemingly boundless plateau of Hamadan, I felt glad to have been born with human faculties, to have seen a little of what is possible in creatures of my kind; that it stayed to warm my spirit, this reflection of a measureless grandeur, as we continued our protracted journey, climbing again into the coloured mountains which guard the pass of Asadabad, descending by Darius's highway through the breakneck windings of the Pai-Tak gorge, down to the hot sand of the Mesopotamian plain.

R.C.H. was delighted with the favourable reaction that the novel received from the Polish community. In February 1953, Z.A. Broncel produced a programme about *Recollection* for the BBC Polish service. This sparked so much interest that Broncel was asked to translate a chapter to be read at a meeting of the Union of Polish Writers abroad. This resulted in a further request from the Polish Catholic émigré weekly, *Zycie* (Life), for a translation of an extract from the novel to appear in an issue about the condition of Poles in Russia. The passage, quoted above, describing the deportation of Poles by train was suggested.

He also received an encouraging letter from Rupert Hart-Davis who had heard that R.C.H. might be leaving Cassells, and asked if he might be allowed to publish him as 'for more than twenty years I have thought of you as the greatest living novelist'. In fact R.C.H. was to move to Geoffrey Bles, but Hart-Davis wrote that 'I will wait patiently, still nursing the unconquerable hope that one day I shall have the honour and joy of being your publisher.' R.C.H. was honoured and delighted by the approach but Hart-Davis' patience was never rewarded.

Another pleasing letter was from a friend Norah Hill, quoting from a letter she had received from the celebrated biographer of the Brontës, Winifred Gerin, who enthusiastically recorded that:

> Recently I read one of my favourite R.C. Hutchinson's newer novels, *Recollection of a Journey,* which, like all his others, I thought wholly admirable. He is a great man – so penetrating of the human heart and so feeling for this century's predicament. He stands alone among English writers for his deep understanding of the continental soul – one might say of the universal soul. I have been reading quite a lot of our best contemporary writers – C.P. Snow, Elizabeth Bowen, etc. and fine as they are, they all seem so limited when compared to R.C. Hutchinson.

Stephen Spender shared this high opinion of *Recollection*, particularly agreeing on R.C.H.'s ability to extend his novels beyond the realm of the lives of the characters to capture the wider society in which they move. One might see each war-based novel as a piece of a jigsaw which when all fitted together constitutes a picture of Europe during the first half of the twentieth century. Spender wrote in the pages of *The Listener* that *Recollection* is 'a wonderful vindication of the power of the novel to hold up the mirror to the most confusing events of our time' and that Hutchinson 'establishes a bridge between our own lives and those of people who have lived in the worst hell of our time'. He sees Hutchinson as being able to combine the realism of Flaubert with the fantasy of Kafka and has the humanity to break through 'the shell of his own personal experience and enter a kind of objective sympathy with a world wider than himself. He enlarges our sense of what is meant by others.' Similar observations were made by an anoymous reviewer in the New York Times, 'Seldom does an author catch such a flashing insight into the central core of human existence'. There can be no greater affirmation of R.C.H.'s achievement in *Recollection of a Journey* than the concluding sentence of the review in the *Observer*: 'I doubt whether in all literature there could be a greater monolith to human misery and endurance.'

In all R.C.H's imaginative travels across Europe it would have been surprising if his eyes had not been drawn to Trieste in the 1940s. After three years of Nazi and Yugoslav occupation, following 'The Trieste Operation' (the 'Liberation of Trieste') of 1945, it was ruled by an Anglo-American military government from 1945 to 1954, while Yugoslavia and Italy wrangled over its future.

In such a volatile theatre of opposing political hopes and fears and desires for revenge, R.C.H. recognized fruitful soil for a novel based on the dangerous world of conflicting loyalties – personal, political, romantic, and moral. It was an ideal world for such a kaleidoscope of emotions and motives: the worlds of Conrad and Graham Greene happily cross-fertilised.

The novel, *March the Ninth*, revolves around these worlds of conflicting desires and loyalties. Eugen Reichenbach is a naturalised American, an idealist surgeon from pre-war Vienna, now working for a World Relief Organisation in Trieste. In an apparently chance meeting, an old acquaintance in Vienna, Kurt Wenzel (who considers himself to be of pure German blood but is in fact, appropriately, a mixture of Jewish, Polish, Hungarian, Slav, Spanish, and Turkish origin), asks for Eugen's help to operate on a Swiss friend who has been shot in an accident. It quickly becomes obvious that this is an absurd cover for a request to save the life of a previous Nazi Commander, Zempelmarck, who is responsible for the massacre of twenty innocent civilians in Bosnia (an incident cruelly familiar to readers decades later). Eugen is subjected to dangerous excursions through remote hilly locations, mostly in semi-serviceable lorries, following, as a virtual prisoner, his patient who is on the run from pursuing partisans eager for revenge. He is accompanied by one of R.C.H.'s most memorable characters, the swashbuckling army doctor, acting as Eugen's anaesthetist, the ever-singing, talking, cannabis-smoking Babitch.

Eugen is thus confronted with two immediate moral dilemmas – one is the obvious political one. He is forced to save the life of a committed Nazi criminal who has no regrets about his past actions. Zempelmarck believes fanatically in his view of patriotism and power:

What do lawyers know about the necessities of war! They
think you can control people by pinning up regulations on
a notice-board. A beautiful notion! Unfortunately real life
is not like that. We who've had the actual experience, we
know there are just two instruments of control – force and
fear … The people who have a right to govern are those
who *can*. Always, in every circumstance! It's only when that
principle's accepted that you get order and peace – which is
what everyone really wants, however much the underlings
may twitter and mumble. The one unforgiveable thing is to
use one's power timidly.

Having to treat a person with these beliefs is one problem for Eugen,
but it is of course combined with his ethical obligations as a doctor.
(We will return to this aspect in the following chapter.) This is also
complicated by his growing understanding of Zempelmarck's position,
however distasteful his beliefs may be. This troubles Eugen's conscience,
and he is disturbed by a remark from Zempelmarck's equally fanatical
sister Paula, who after they have been thrown together after an attack
on their vehicle, whispered 'a remark of which I should have thought
herself incapable: You and I, Dr. Reichenbach, we make curious journeys
together!'

But there is a stronger moral dilemma to confuse Eugen's
conscience. He has fallen in love with Zempelmarck's wife, Franzisza.
He admires her loyalty and they are drawn together by their equally
strong moral and personal impulses. (It is intriguing to surmise who
Franziska was in R.C.H.'s imagination, for there is an unpublished
short story of the same title.) A central paragraph describes Eugen's
confusions entailed by his visits to treat Zempelmarck at Vischak,
combined with these being visits to Franzisza:

For, as I see now, I was already and finally committed.
Not by reason or conscience: I had ceased to argue that I
was tied to these visits by professional obligation. In truth,
I believe that such decisions are to be traced to a region
of the spirit where the voices of self-interest and morality
alike are silent. I had made no promise to Franzizska;
but my constant return to Vischak surely implied that I
was bound to her cause, and I had almost ceased to ask
myself what elements of right and wrong that cause might

embrace. Enough that it was hers. We do not, I think, select our loyalties. We march behind men's flags because of their power and confidence: I followed a woman's, finding in her powerlessness, as well as in her goodness, a compulsion against which I myself was powerless.

Zempelmarck is eventually captured and subjected to a kangaroo court which condemns him to be shot on the anniversary of the original massacre, 9 March. The problem is that Zempelmarck is now virtually beyond medical help and Eugen is seen as an accomplice and is commanded to keep him alive and if necessary to hold him in position for his execution. The novel ends with unexpected consequences for all concerned.

The novel was the most successful post-war novel in commercial terms, earning altogether over £3,000 between 1957 and 1960. But this was nonetheless a modest amount, considering that in 1922 this amount would have been equivalent to circa £55,000. As is true of so many of the novels, it is vividly visual in its impact. The financial income included a generous film option from Twentieth Century Fox, but nothing materialised. There was also a three-act television adaptation, written by Elizabeth Lincoln, for Associated Rediffusion, but it was never broadcast. As ever, many readers who were familiar with Trieste found it very difficult to believe that it was written by someone who had never visited the city.

In his obituary of R.C.H., Rupert Hart-Davis suggested that at least seven of the novels were 'major works, fit to stand beside the finest novels of the century'. He did not name them – and every novel has found its particular advocates – but it would be surprising if the four post-war novels referred to above were not on his list. One title, however, we can be confident was in his mind: the epic novel about the Bolshevik revolution, which brought R.C.H. his first taste of prominence and public admiration, *Testament*. It is always difficult to remember that it was composed entirely in his study in Birdlip – except for visits to the reference section of the local public library – when he was in his early thirties and had rarely ventured further afield than Southern England.

Any reviewer of a novel as huge as *Testament* faces an almost impossible task, simply because it covers over 700 pages and contains a multitude of characters. (R.C.H. claimed that it took him 2,000 hours to write.) A lengthy fictional preface explains that the author is recording a virtually unedited translation of an account written by a survivor of the events, Captain Alexei Otraveskov, and his friendship with a lawyer and fellow soldier, Count Anton Scheffler. It is around the developing intense relationship between these two main characters that the novel revolves.

It is inevitable that comparisons are made between *War and Peace* and *Testament* and R.C.H. certainly constructs the novel as though it was a Russian epic – even including a list of the 51 main characters as an appendix, recording their formal addresses, patronyms, and family names, so the reader can cope with (for example) the fact that Scheffler's wife may be referred to as Yelisaveta Akinievna, sometimes called 'The Little Princess', 'The Countess', 'Lisveta', 'Vetrisha'. There is, however, a distinct difference between Tolstoy's narrative stance and Hutchinson's. *War and Peace* keeps the two elements of the title mostly in separate compartments, often confined to consecutive chapters; *Testament* is a typically Hutchinsonian evolving narrative with its varying elements intrinsically intermingled throughout. A look at the origins of the novel may act as a guide to the major strands of the narrative.

In a letter to Ernest Raymond in October 1939, R.C.H. wrote about the initial planning:

> Before I began writing I bought (for one shilling) a book about Russia written by a prosy little Scotsman and published in 1860. For the rest, I found in Cheltenham library several padded journals, mostly by woolly and slightly hysterical ladies who ran like hell out of Petrogad (small blame to them) as soon as Kerensky [Prime Minister in 1917] came into view … a few hours dipping about in these sloppy little backwaters of the book world gives one a complete picture of an epoch – though I must doubt if it's anything like a correct picture!

Had R.C.H. forgotten what he wrote, aged 13, in a letter to his mother about hearing a talk given at school evening prayers: 'He spoke on the religious side of Bolshevistic Russia. It was awfully interesting though very terrible, and gave us an idea of the conditions out there.'

Three elements can be extracted from these two reminiscences: the novel aims to give 'a complete picture of an epoch'; it was to try to capture this through the lives of ordinary people (even if they are 'woolly and slightly hysterical ladies') and their 'terrible conditions'; and it was to explore the moral and 'religious side of Bolshevistic Russia'.

In terms of painting 'a complete picture of an epoch', R.C.H. certainly succeeded in giving the reader an overview of the changing loyalties and conflicting extremes of propaganda which oppressed the Russian people. At times some could not understand which side of the conflict they were thought to support. Loyalties could divide families – Otraveskov's sister, Katie, is a committed communist who describes her brother as 'an epitome of lukewarm intellectual benevolence without direction'. In a prolonged discussion on the ambiguous nature of revolution, Otraveskov hears the views of a general who regrets what has been lost:

> In the new existence we are shaping, much will be lost that has a kind of aesthetic value: the slow rhythm of our country life; the idleness of the privileged from which we have developed a mellow philosophy; our imperial pageantry; the intimate relationship, understood so perfectly, between the man who loves his land and the men who till it. All that has to go.

But the future offers:

> A gigantic harvest in human happiness from the freedom suddenly bestowed on us. We have, for instance, the rudiments of a system of justice which will reach the special needs of our temperament ... More important still, we have here in Petrograd men with enough political experience and constructive imagination to get the whole machinery of progress into working order ... My one terror is that men of another kind, irresponsible demagogues who think of nothing but sweeping away our entire economic and social fabric overnight ... Capitulation, turmoil, anarchy: is that all we are to get in return for two million lives?

Otraveskov asks him how wars are won. The reply is the opposite of Zempelmarck's view in *March the Ninth* ('force and fear'): "'I don't know", he said meditatively. "Battles are won by two things, love and fear." "And hitherto there has been insufficient love," I said.'

The whole confusion comes to a head in the character of Scheffler, who having been seen as a resolute ally of the proletariat is put on trial and is then tried and condemned as a Czarist counter-revolutionary. We are presented with the words of the wife of the Secretary of the Political Department of the Judicial Committee, who explains why Scheffler is on trial (she herself had been, in the past, arrested as a suspected assassin):

> It is not because he has challenged *us*, it is because he has challenged the thing we have lived for, the thing I was nearly hanged for. Count Scheffler ... hunts to find good in malicious people, he becomes attached to people who are dangerous. With him it is always the individual who matters. He cannot think of the millions who have suffered and will go on suffering if we allow the acquisitive and cruel to have their way again. He is a lawyer, he thinks in terms of particular cases, he is simply unable to picture the great march of liberation.

Scheffler represents all the confusions and tensions that trouble Otraveskov's mind, but he becomes something like a hero for him. He is a figure of idealism, a pursuer of justice, a stubborn believer in intellectual freedom, a fervent humanitarian (though his stubbornness is not always an attractive trait for the reader, and his idealism can sometimes lead to almost suicidal intransigence). He is also a devout Roman Catholic (and the novel's title encourages us to consider this aspect together with all the other strands of the story). He offers us the opposite view to Katie's friend Volodya who, when asked if he believes in God, replies:

> Yes – in God, or in destiny, I don't mind which name you use, but 'destiny' seems to me more polite. It is 'God', if you prefer that word, who has conducted the affairs of mankind up till now, God who with infinite slowness and cynical indifference has been working out what the theologians call 'His Purpose', vague as that purpose seems to be ... God is the supreme evil, the eternal enemy, eternally regretting that he gave man Reason with which to oppose his callous

plans. That is what we are fighting, that is the task of our generation: to fight against God, to thwart him and turn him out.

But for Scheffler it is the opposite. In a moving letter to Otraveskov, as he prepares to face the court's sentence, he writes:

> Sorry the writing's bad. Someone got wind that I was writing , they have broken the fingers of my right hand to stop it and I am using my left ... I don't know what has happened to me, I can't understand the clearness I see with now. I thought that all that I had tried to do was wasted ... the joys have come back to me, far more beautiful now that my eyes are cleared ... I hear them getting ready, it will only be half an hour now. Such happiness, such perfect, burning happiness ... I am filled and held and covered with the sweeping blazing love of Jesus.

Scheffler's jovial servant Yevski (who, ever-smiling, constantly appears to rescue Scheffler at moments of near disaster, and has some of the memorable characteristics of Babitch in *March the Ninth*) reports on Scheffler's final moments: 'They wheeled him out in his chair – he couldn't stand up, see? Two rounds they put in him – four rifles that was – they took off his bandage, and he looked at them ... and ... they saw him grin ... they finished him off with their butts.'

Throughout *Testament*, R.C.H. constantly continues to show his ability to capture a feeling of communal suffering by his skill in describing crowd scenes as each single scene adds to the creation of a wide panorama, using his pen like a roaming camera. We have seen this power at work in *The Unforgotten Prisoner* (which might be seen in some ways as a first draft for *Testament*), but here it is extended as we are given portrayals of crowds being violently attacked for being on the 'wrong' side, horses being driven callously through groups of disenfranchised, homeless 'agitators', women being beheaded, train-drivers shot for not moving broken-down engines, old bourgeois (having had their houses appropriated) reduced to homeless poverty. These are interwoven with vivid scenes of wounded prisoners in overcrowded, insanitary field hospitals where one can almost smell the aroma of impending death. In an extraordinary description of half-alive returning soldiers 'on the march', he manages to sustain a pathetic picture of tortured bodies, defiantly refusing to surrender to their physical misery in a macabre, black comedy as though the spectators were watching a puppet show:

> The procession was not a good one, as processions went, it seemed to have no banners and no cohesion. The men who could walk marched rather sleepily and with a certain shyness, as captives must have marched in a Roman triumph; they came ten deep, but the ranks were most irregular, for a man would pause to light a cigarette and never trouble to get in line again. The legless, or one-legged, came next behind them, carried on anything with wheels, chairs, barrows, even a perambulator. These were more cheerful than the walkers, though they must have been far colder; one that I noticed was smiling and bowing to friends he saw in the crowd, pointing in a humorous way to his knees, where his body ended. He, I remember, was wheeled by a man totally blind, and he seemed to find it enormously amusing when his chair collided at every few paces with those going along beside it. It must have taken nearly ten minutes to pass, this part of the procession ... but behind was still the line of 'totally disabled', nearly as long again. Of these men you saw very little – a shape on a stretcher, that was really all... Among these stretchers there were walking cases which seemed to have been arranged with a certain artistry, as a stamp-collector places his specimens: a blinded man, supported on one side, came hopping on one leg; behind him, a man with no arms; next, one who turned his head from side to side as he walked and at every turn stretched his mouth wide open in a hideous smile; then a man with his head thrown right back, a position he could not alter, and after that one whose face, black and unbandaged, showed no feature that you could label eye or nose or mouth. Last of all a cart came by, a low wagon without sides such as they use for builders' battens, and on this the cases had been posed with ingenious skill to show their mutilation: a trunk without either arms or legs but with a face alive and stretched with pain; a man with a single leg, no other limbs; a legless man with half his

face burnt away, who (deliberately as it appeared) slowly opened and closed his single eye to show he was living. The crowd received this spectacle in silence.

Another repeated demonstration of authorial craft is R.C.H.'s ability to create authentic, realistic moments in entirely imagined settings. Jonty Driver (writer, poet, and former headmaster) highlighted this in a perceptive review of *Testament*. Driver had experienced solitary confinement in South Africa in the 1960s as a result of anti-apartheid activity as a student. He described the interrogation and detention that Otraveskov has to endure as being evoked with 'a dramatic vividness unsurpassed by anything else I have read'.

The novel is not, of course, written entirely in dark tones. There are tender moments throughout – particularly in the sometimes puzzling relationship between Scheffler and his wife, and in Otraveskov's love for his own troubled, neurotic wife, Natalia, and their joint devotion to their crippled son, Ivan. Indeed the novel ends with daylight breaking on Otraveskov and Natalia, even if it is breaking on earthly separation, for they had pledged to each other that 'there's nowhere my spirit can go where your love won't find me'. It is a fitting 'testament' to the power of love.

With the award of the *Sunday Times* medal for fiction, *Testament* assured R.C.H. of at least a few years of public recognition. He didn't collect the medal in person, claiming that he was too deeply immersed in the next novel but perhaps it was just innate shyness. It was warmly received by a host of foremost reviewers (and cemented a friendship with Eddie Sackville-West, to whom the novel is dedicated) and was quickly translated into Swedish, German, Norwegian, French, and Spanish. No Russian version was to materialise. Sir Newman Flower, Director of Cassells, wrote to R.C.H. in 1942 that 'the terrible thing to me is the paper shortage has prohibited our reprinting *Testament*. I could have sold 200,000 now, if the Govt. would give us the paper.'

The popularity of *Testament* continued through the 1950s and then began to fade. It has never failed, however, to be discovered by dedicated readers. Recent enthusiasts have included the eminent cellist, Steven Isserlis, who described it as 'a searing read, at times almost unbearable, but it's irresistible'. Perhaps the most appropriate way to end an overview of R.C.H. and war, and *Testament* in particular, is to quote a review contributed to the internet by an author describing himself just as 'Robin', who decided that the best way to describe *Testament* was simply to compile a list of just twenty-three appropriate words, suggesting that it was a novel about: 'War, dread, suffering, farce, friendship, idealism, justice, tragedy, longing, love, daring, courage, self-denial, beauty, kindness, betrayal, evil, revolution, order, chaos, terror, horror and hope!'

R.C.H. and Margaret with Lord and Lady Oaksey,
Nuremberg.

The cover image for *Recollection
of a Journey*, 1952, showing Polish
refugees being deported by train.

R.C.H. and Margaret, 1945.

Chapter 6

R.C.H. and Medicine

Nearly all R.C.H.'s novels make reference to medicine in some way or other – in several cases it concerns the central character, sometimes a fringe character, sometimes just a passing reference within the plot. Yet R.C.H. had no family connection with medicine and it is difficult to know why it played such a central role in his imagination.

There is a definite progression in his interest in seeing humans in terms of their physical bodies. He shared Dickens' obsession with physical deformities, R.C.H.'s novels including – from the very first novel – figures such as the disabled, hunch-backs, or amputees. Gradually these develop from passing 'extras' in his cast to those suffering physical disabilities as casualties of war. He then turns to a more intense pre-occupation with mental and psychological sufferings – frequently the result of wartime experiences.

R.C.H. had his own share of medical problems, from a weak heart as a child, which developed into more serious angina, and he was troubled with back strain. But he treated his own discomforts with typical nonchalance – his description of visiting a heart specialist in London in 1970 is amusingly described in a letter to Martyn Skinner:

> In the vast Queen Anne drawing-room where he works, with machinery discreetly placed behind the Ming vases and the Adam commodes, when he had arranged me half-naked on a luxuriously upholstered slab, a sort of priestess glided softly in – without any gong or tucket sounding, believe it or not – bearing four little chains on a silver

tray. These she attached to my wrists and ankles, and then squeezed some sacred ointment in small blobs on my chest. 'All is ready, Doggins,' she cried, and he linked the chains with a sort of mystic cabinet. 'One more blob,' he said, 'on the starboard side.' 'Aye, aye, Guru Sahib.' 'Stand By!' He then put on coloured eye-masks, bells discreetly rang, lights twinkled. I *think* I heard a distant voice say melodiously, 'Oh, all ye computers, bless ye the Lord, praise him and magnify him for ever' ... When it was all over, both dogginses said ... 'That's what *you've* got,' answering grimly, poring over cardiac charts and x-ray photographs. However I got them to compromise: for the next few weeks – possibly months – I am to behave like one of Madame Tussaud's creations. I am not to mow lawns, or run, or (except if the house catches fire) walk. I am to go to bed early, rise late, rest at midday. Food to be altogether avoided ... If I *faithfully* follow this programme I may be back to normal, they say, before the close of 1971, so it seems worth trying, as I want to write another book or two.

He quickly began to take an interest in the specific details of medical procedures. Interestingly, he confided (again to Martyn Skinner):

Psychologically, the thing is odd. As example: I could not, without fainting read the description of a surgical operation; I am one of those persons of effeminate neurological set-up whom the sight of a cut finger makes queasy. Yet when, for a professional purpose, I spent an hour cross-examining a surgeon about the details of an operation, not one hair turned.

He would have been able to consult his old school friend and doctor, Jeremy Churchill, but he went further and paid for a retired doctor and surgeon to visit him for 'tutorials' on medical practice – another careful attention to detail when introducing medical procedures in his novels, such as the hospital visits of Otraveskov on behalf of his crippled son in *Testament*, and in particular the surgical operations of Eugen Reichenbach in *March the Ninth*. To add to the more obscure vocabulary that we have seen spread through the novels, R.C.H. now adds medical vocabulary as though it was in daily household usage:

staphylococci, laryngeal, keloid, oedema, leucocytes, oligophrenia, ament. In *Testament,* Otraveskov discusses with his doctor the ideas of Weir Mitchell (often seen as the 'father' of medical neurology, and satirised by Virginia Woolf in *Mrs Dalloway*), and in *March the Ninth* Eugen makes an investigation of the periosteum and considers possible mediastinal incision, while Babitch makes use of an apparent modification of Guthjahr's apparatus before administering procaine.

It was inevitable that R.C.H.'s medical interests would extend to the moral aspects implicit in clinical procedure. Such conflicts nicely mirrored the moral dilemmas experienced by Eugen in *March the Ninth* and Josef in *The Fire and the Wood* as they struggled with their duties as doctors acting under the obligations of the Hippocratic Oath and their individual desires: medical knowledge (in Josef's case) or political and humane ideals (in Eugen's case). Perhaps the pivotal sentence in *March the Ninth* is: 'We do not, I think, select our loyalties. We march behind men's flags because of their power and confidence.' The conflicts that Josef and Eugen experience is reflected in the conflicts of loyalties experienced in the romantic lives of many of R.C.H.'s characters and in the lives of several of his military figures.

The novel which focuses on the moral ambiguities of medical research is *The Fire and the Wood.* Here, Josef's obsessive desire to find a cure for tuberculosis threatens to suffocate his human feelings as his chronically suffering patients become close to being 'specimens' rather than individuals. One of his fellow doctors observes: 'young Zeppichmann never did think of the patients' comfort, except where comfort had a physiological importance', and when three rats die after being injected with an experimental drug by Josef, he muses:

> What if a human subject went off like that ... But it was a case of one life against thousands. Somewhere, in a newspaper, he had come across a phrase used by a political speaker. 'It is the many that we have to think of. The individual doesn't matter.' Yes, that was it. *The individual doesn't matter.*

It is surprising that no reviewer referred to the unusual title and its possible significance. It must, surely, evoke the biblical story of Abraham and Isaac, which R.C.H. would almost certainly have been familiar with from his Crusader classes as a teenager. Abraham's faith is put to the ultimate test when God orders him to sacrifice his son Isaac – to build an altar and make a 'burnt offering'. Abraham does so and Isaac calls to his father: 'Behold the fire and the wood: but where is the lamb for sacrifice?' Abraham explains that Isaac is to be the sacrifice and prepares to perform the act, but his obedience is rewarded by the sacrifice being stopped at the final moment. Josef takes on the role of Abraham in being involuntarily tested as to how far he will sacrifice individual patients for his ideal – to find a cure that could save a huge number of lives from a vicious disease. He decides to light the fire which will ignite the wood to perform this sacrifice, until he has to reassess his actions through his love for Minna. How successfully his sacrifice is averted or achieved is left to the reader to decide.

A novel he was working on between *The Fire and the Wood* and *March the Ninth* was *The Stepmother*. One recalls the words in R.C.H.'s Monkton diary: 'I think one day … I shall write a novel on the parent problem', and two other entries: 'I want one day to write a novel exposing happiness' and 'There is another thing I want to do. That is to write a novel illustrating this wild chase after happiness which constitutes an important part of our existence.' One imagines that this vision of happiness centred on a thirst for economic security (at age 16, he was going through his phase of investigating socialism) but in 1952 he was more interested in the ideas of inner psychological 'happiness' and was considering how this might be combined with thoughts of parenthood – *The Stepmother* became the vessel for this distillation. It is difficult not to feel that these ideas spring from his own childhood images of his mother who became a stepmother a few years younger than Catherine in the novel, though Mabel was the stepmother of a 4-year-old son while Catherine became the stepmother of an adult son. But the figure of his mother must surely have been in R.C.H.'s mind in the dedication of the novel to his elder daughter Ann, specifically calling her Ann Coryton Hutchinson, evoking his mother's maiden name Coryton. Stephen, in the novel, is convinced that his mother's hunting accident, confining her to a wheelchair, caused paralysis resulting in difficulties in child-bearing; R.C.H.'s father's first wife, also called Catherine, died after complications giving birth to R.C.H.'s step-brother, Sheldon. Any autobiographical influences end at this point.

Some reviewers made comparisons with Daphne du Maurier's *Rebecca*, but although there is the obvious similarity of a second marriage and its confusions, there is nothing gothic about *The Stepmother* and R.C.H. had never read *Rebecca*. *The Stepmother* is one of R.C.H.'s most poetic novels, the prose moving with finely musical rhythms. The work is unusually short, consisting of 32 chapters compressed into just over 200 pages. It is an atmospheric novel, seen mostly through Catherine's acute but troubled eyes. The dominant image is that of a stage with many references to the 'parts' characters are playing, the author being a stage manager adjusting sets, costumes, and make-up, and the reader joins the characters moving through different rooms, feeling the furniture as if they were physically touching it, inhaling the smells, hearing the sounds, vividly aware of the texture of their own clothes and the dress of others. Vere, Stephen's fiancée, works for a theatrical company, her life 'belonged to the arid back rooms of the theatre'. The family home, Gunners, into which Catherine is thrust, is cold and austere like its owner Lawrence, and becomes a character within the drama. The novel has much in common with E.M. Forster's *Howards End*, both in terms of the symbolism of the house and the internal inhibitions of the inhabitants, even though the settings are divided by two wars, the one anticipating conflict and the other recovering from it. The problems confronting Saggard in *The Unforgotten Prisoner* confront Stephen as well. Stifled conversations at the dinner table at Gunners are painfully but amusingly captured as Catherine has to struggle with her responsibilities as a 'mother' and (importantly, she is childless) which pose anxieties as to whether her role is one of duty or affection, one of fulfilment or sacrifice – and can either satisfy happiness? Can she combine her role as mother with that of wife, and does she, at heart, feel one is more important than the other? Can either role be a true expression of love or happiness, or is it a striving for gratitude? (One chapter opens with the question: 'Gratitude?'). Her first challenge is to face the apparently emotionless Stephen, though cruelty often seems ready to burst out from his coldness – poignantly captured in the contrast of the look in Stephen's eyes with that shown in the portrait of his mother, Josie (there is to be a portrait of Catherine to compare later): 'Lottie had said that Stephen's eyes were like Josie's. But the warmth of light in Josie's eyes was not in these. It had been said of Josie that as she looked at your face she seemed to come towards you. This man surveyed you from a great way off.' Catherine's problems are concentrated by the constant presence of Josie's portrait looking down at her. She knows that she cannot view her situation as a competition with a dead person, yet she cannot totally prevent herself from doing so: 'I shan't try to be another Josie. I realise I couldn't ever be that to Lawrence...but if I am in no sense to take Josie's place' she thought 'what am I doing here at all?' Catherine's inner tensions can be focussed on the problem of how to make a house a home, and she realised early that for the family there was no division between the two: 'She had realised almost in the first hour that an organism of such complexity would not easily suffer grafting. It derived from many lives. Lawrence, growing here, had learnt it as a child learns his own language. He belonged to it as he would never belong to her.' And so Catherine found 'herself' *outside* rather than *inside* Gunners – in the garden: 'In July! Yes, in July the garden would show an unimaginable splendour – but to whom?' Catherine, born in Canada, but educated in Germany, describes her first impression of an English rural autumn, though the vision was tinged with melancholy:

> Here was something new to her experience, this wealth of gauzed sunlight, the stillness, the subtle breath of English woodland quickened by early frost; yet she could feel, as if she had lived here through the seasons, that the gentleness of light and air only disguised the summer's passing. The year was elderly. Catching its mood, the sense of strength beginning to waste, she found it foolish to have thought that at forty-six one might still look forward to harvest.

As Catherine nursed Lawrence through his final illness, the ice in Lawrence's emotions began to thaw, but though it provided some of the closeness she was striving for, it also gave rise to more complications than she was prepared for.

There are several moments of tenderness in the novel but the core of it concentrates on the inner unhappiness of Catherine. One defining moment is her despair at Stephen's apparent lack of any human sympathy: 'the man beside her ceased to be an individual ... it's only when you get old you realise what hell means – it's looking inside yourself and finding there's nothing there, only a cocoon of egotism and conceit, nothing that anyone could possibly love.' This bleak picture of egotism had been a life-long concern of R.C.H. (he describes himself theatrically at least seven times in his schoolboy diary as 'egotistic' and 'self-centred') and it was to find its expression in what might be seen as the twin novel to *The Stepmother*, the remarkable and searing description of this mental state in *Image of My Father*, written four years after *The Stepmother*.

In the figure of Vincent Levesque we are confronted with a broad portrayal of a character who has lost all sense of purpose in life – disillusioned by his experience of war, by religion, by all concepts of affection (suffering from his wife's desertion) and whose only motivation lies in survival – and only if that has the possibility of resulting in some personal advantage. We first meet Vincent in a desolate corner of Poland in 1944. Here, this tall, bearded, thin, physically strong Belgian is part of a forced labour unit of the retreating German army, all hungry, sparsely clothed, engaged in dragging oil drums and timber through freezing and biting snow, all in preparation to effect a scorched-earth policy to halt the pursuing Russian army. It is Vincent who rushes into the neighbouring village to attempt to rescue the abandoned inhabitants and carried a dead girl over his shoulders to the refuge of a ruined church; but he is also the person who later that night is seen strangling the already dead girl with a coil of wire. This deeply troubled, highly intelligent, tormented, haunted character becomes the focus of the novel through over 400 compelling pages.

Vincent's obsession that each individual must selfishly find their own purpose in life is linked to a firm belief in the power of one's genetic inheritance – we are who we are because of our past – and he is beset with problems concerning his own origins. He knows that he is illegitimate but knows nothing about his natural parents. His mission to discover the truth about his past is in part a search for identity and in part a desire to be released from the religious strictures which he has been brought up with – he deeply resents that he has been made to feel that his life is a series of acts of penitence (back to Klaus's penitence chamber) for a past which has been hidden from him. He longs to be released from the 'humiliation of bastardy' and this resentment is personified in his antipathy to his teacher-priest, Abbé Bernier, and is extended to a rejection of religion and all moral concepts of right and wrong, which he dismisses as platitudes. The horrors of war have crystallised this for him: 'As for goodness, I come to realise that that's an invention of Bernier and his kind. In the real world there is no such thing.' As to evil, 'I learnt it for myself these last years. All of it! And not out of textbooks, as he has.'

These convictions are married to his journeying into his past: 'It's no use your telling me God made me – I want to know what man and woman were responsible. How can I think of God's intentions when I don't even know theirs! I want to know who I am!'

Vincent's long, dark journey to discover the identity of his father could hardly have been more full of obstacles. Like Dickens' Oliver, he is supported by a mysterious benefactor, regularly enhancing his bank balance and then naming him as his heir. After much investigation Vincent discovers that this benefactor, David Selborne, may well be his father – a rich industrialist, an infamously harsh employer, a total 'egoist'. Unfortunately, the Selborne family dispute Selborne's wills (there are three of them) and believe that David Selborne died childless and left his fortune to his nephew. After endless legal disputes, Vincent – who has been living in Selborne's house under an assumed name – claims his inheritance. He worships the memory, the 'image' of his father, who achieved his position and wealth by hard work and rejection of any emotional feelings. 'Business' is everything; it produces 'employment, wine and bootlaces'. Vincent declares: 'There is only one remedy – to cut yourself from everything which is battening on your softness. You've got to deal with other people – that's necessary for your livelihood – but there's no need to be implicated in their feelings. They can look after themselves.' It was in Vincent's power, he believed, to become what his father had been.

Yet there is another impulse within Vincent which he cannot 'strangle', for his love for his wife Germaine remains however much he claims to be free from such romantic fantasies. He revisited the strangling of the girl in the Polish church in a nightmare where the girl is transformed into Germaine. He cannot allow himself to accept the affection of his natural mother, who has become a devout nurse to mentally deranged women. In despair she tells him that there is no help she can give him in his emotionally sterile world: 'I shall pray for you … It's all there is left for me to do.' But there is another woman whom he cannot reject – his 'cousin' Ruth, who has found a heart within Vincent but who will not agree to any relationship because she believes he should return to Germaine. She leaves him with the sad farewell: 'I shall pray for you – always!' In despair, Vincent exclaims: '"I shall pray for you": that dreaded valediction of women, that desolate refrain!'

One reviewer suggested that the novel was reminiscent of Mauriac in one of his grimmer moods, and it certainly enters the dark night of Vincent's soul. But it takes the reader on this sometimes frightening path with a sense of sympathy and increasing understanding throughout the narrative. There is an ever-present sense of potential violence surrounding Vincent from the opening scene in the deserted church, in his confrontation with Germaine's lover, and in his final visit to Germaine as he faces the final confrontation with his demons – he stands over the sleeping Germaine, but one of his hands is fingering a coil of wire in his pocket.

In many ways the three novels – *The Stepmother, Johanna at Daybreak, Image of My Father* (and to some extent *Recollections of a Journey*) – are all linked by the problems of how one's past impinges on one's present and how one can escape from the confines of one's past (perhaps false) memories. Vincent and Catherine come to share Johanna's declaration: 'No one's life can be divided into past and present with a thick line ruled between the two.' They all have to face the problem posed at the end of *The Stepmother* by Lawrence's question: 'If people are only what chance makes them – if they're only the result of a psychological equation, I don't see what there is to believe in.' The answer seems to come from the voice of Vincent's mother, when in reply to his declaration about her patients that 'There's nothing here, after all – no human individual, no creature with its own will, nothing but a bundle of appetites and senseless reactions', she responds that if he thinks that: 'You are always, always wrong.' Vincent needed to discard his 'image' of his father and the importance of material inheritance to discover what his inheritance could provide – a journey towards a moral sense of a world not just dependent on 'wine and bootlaces' but a vision based on love and shared humanity. It was not just a sudden insight, like a Damascus road experience, but a gradual and painful realisation. The natural history of this Selborne took him to a tearful understanding (as always with R.C.H., it was the beginning of a journey, not a conclusion) that he was about to join 'a vast, warm stream … sweeping through the dam of vanities, of self-absorption and self-distrust which has seemed so long to be his sole defence … he felt himself to be outside time and space … in a fire of joy which was outside his understanding, which he did not need to understand.'

R.C.H. would have been pleased to read the acute comments in a review of the novel in the *Saturday Review*, which described Hutchinson as an 'eminently civilized man who can chart a course to sanity through violence, madness and despair. His characters never dissolve into sentimentality because he accepts the limits imposed by inheritance and environment on their freedom to change their natures. This basic rationality makes his monsters credible and his saints sympathetic.'

A further exploration into the medical field which strongly affected R.C.H. both professionally and personally was to provide the origins of one of his most influential novels, *A Child Possessed*. He wrote about how the novel formed in his mind and it is worth quoting at some length:

> The germ of a novel arrives, I believe, in one moment of intense experience … With me the moment is generally lost even before the work begins. To the question: 'What gave you the idea for that story?' the answer as a rule is, 'I really don't know.' But by chance I can trace the source of *A Child Possessed*. Some talented and charming friends of mine had an only son who was classified as a low-grade mongol. Once, when he was four or five years old, they placed him for a fortnight in a private institution which cared for such children, so that they themselves might have a holiday; and while he was there it occurred to me to visit him. There was no hope of his recognizing me, but I vaguely thought that if he seemed contented my independent account might reassure his parents. The expedition failed in its purpose: the boy happened to be sound asleep when I arrived, and it was thought a pity to disturb him; so the only report I could send his mother was at second-hand. That episode was a very small one, but because of a few seconds within it the experience became part of the mental lumber which one never quite abandons. When I arrived the matron was busy and I was taken through the house to wait for her in the garden. Not far from where I sat, four or five children, all of them with what a layman describes as mongoloid features were sitting about in various postures of idleness and apathy: the sight was faintly distressing, and I felt afresh the repugnance which, since my childhood, such creatures had always stirred in me. The matron came, and we sat talking for a few minutes. I think she may have felt that I was unconvinced by her assertion that the boy I had come about was happy; for suddenly, without preamble, she turned and called to one of the children: 'Robert, come and say how-do-you-do to Mr. Hutchinson.' The boy she had called came quickly. I stood up and held out my hand, but his small, slightly malformed one was out first. We shook

hands, I bowing and shyly smiling, he smiling without any such embarrassment. Then he turned away and, I am certain, at once forgot my existence. Another boy was called up in the same fashion, then a little girl, and the trifling ritual was twice repeated. That was all that happened. But each of the three had given me an instantaneous, friendly smile. Do animals smile? A dog, of course, will use eyes and mouth to express delight, recognition, devotion. But I cannot think of an expression on the face of any animal which could be remotely compared with the smiles of those children. I have no means to describe them; indeed it would be dishonest to pretend that my mind's eye will re-create their faces – for I am a poor observer of detail, with an unreliable memory. What I do remember is that, lasting for only a moment, the smile of each of them had a suggestion of eternity: it said to me – I am trying to write objectively – 'I recognize you as a person. You and I belong to the same part of creation.' At the time it did not occur to me that so brief an experience, for all its vitality, would ever interest me professionally. The value of an idea to a novelist is often tested by its power of survival. Years later – somewhere about 1960 – the smiles of those children were still alive in me and the questions they had made me ask myself were revived by one the visits I paid to a big public establishment for the mentally subnormal of all ages. There I watched a young teacher sturdily playing the piano, while another surrounded by a dozen dribbling, blank-faced children, was trying to make them beat time to the music. There was scarcely any response. The dedication, the heroic patience of those two young women – was it all a waste of their gifts, their training and their time? A little later, in the big dining-room, I saw a boy of perhaps eleven years, with idiot eyes, suddenly leave his place to approach a boy at another table: the younger one's face was moustached with jam; the elder picked up a paper napkin, with the quick businesslike kindness of a nanny he wiped the infant's face and then returned to his own chair. Remotely, the incident provided an answer to my question (which has since been more fully answered): the Christ-like devotion of those who care for these children is, (I thought) *never* wasted; for in all of them, in the most vacant, the most repellently ill-shaped, something can happen which we are bound to recognize as human, something which in the end bears witness to the involvement of God in man. From such reflections, joined with a private fondness for the enchantments of Marseilles, Eugénie Stepanovna was born ... In *A Child Possessed* my object was to portray a repulsive creature, apparently mindless, but of the human species, and then to show how one man loved her. In a curious way I found myself eventually sharing in his love.

A Child Possessed asks us to share the extraordinary journey experienced by Stepan, a Russian aristocrat – with a chequered past, including a prison sentence for assault – but living in Marseilles as a lorry driver, under the name of Lopuchine. He is separated from his wife, Hélène, who is a successful actress, travelling the world under the name of Hélène Milescu. Stepan left Hélène soon after the birth of their daughter Eugénie, a severely disabled child unable, it seems, to communicate – without language or any suggestion of reasonable perception.

Stepan had been told that she died, very young, in a mental institution. But life for Stepan changes when he is summoned to a hospital in Switzerland to discover that Eugénie is alive, aged 15. The doctors are convinced that the only hope for Eugénie lies in experimental surgery, with no guarantee of success. Hélène agrees to the operation going ahead – but Stepan refuses to allow his daughter to become a medical 'experiment' (having the opposite views of the value of human life to the youthful Josef's early beliefs in *The Fire and the Wood*), and takes her to live with him. What follows is a deeply moving account of Stepan's growing affection for Eugénie, which develops into devotion – she becomes his constant companion, virtually living in the passenger seat of his long-distance lorry. She becomes Stepan's total obsession, and he believes that he has broken through her barriers of communication. At times, the novel becomes almost unbearable in its poignancy but any sentimentality is suppressed, for it is never clear whether this relationship between father and daughter is a reciprocal one, or lies just in the imagination of Stepan. The important question is posed by the ambiguities inherent in the novel's title. Is Eugénie 'possessed' by an incurable mental disease, or is she the loved 'possession' of Stepan?

The 'medical' novels of R.C.H. in this period have focussed on dissecting the mental problems of the protagonists – Josef, Stephanie, Vincent, Catherine – but in *A Child Possessed* we observe the impact of a child's mental state on her carers, in particular on Stepan. The same problems which afflict the other novels' characters remain, but Stepan has to accept that HE and Hélène are the origins of Eugénie's state – he has not to search the past for answers but to look into himself. When one of Eugénie's doctors declares 'We can't calculate mathematically the value of any life we're concerned with,' Stepan replies: 'On that,' he said thoughtfully, 'I agree.'

In some ways R.C.H. seemed to be living his life in reverse in the 1960s and 1970s, for three of his last four novels are set in places of which he had personal knowledge, rather than imagined ones, and the Marseilles of *A Child Possessed* is a town for which he had acquired a considerable affection. The atmosphere of streets jumbled haphazardly together, the crowded alleys, the smell of the sea, all combine to create the image which Stepan has of Marseilles, both as a place and as a symbol of hope:

> I adore Marseilles. Have you ever seen the very old women in the Place Jean-Jaures? So brave and beautiful. Sometimes I think God meant the Marseillais to be Russians – they accept their lives so gallantly, with so few comforts to feed their courage.

The novel also represents a remarkable biographical episode (but similarly 'reversed') in R.C.H.'s life. Some readers found it difficult to believe that such an arresting account of Eugénie's suffering did not come from some personal experience, and were unsurprised to discover that R.C.H.'s younger son, Piers, had a severely handicapped daughter, Roma. R.C.H. describes the course of events to Martyn Skinner:

> When the mother was worn out Margaret took the wee creature over for four months ... We found her strangely lovable, but she made no progress. Then a most *devoted* foster-mother took her, but despaired after a few weeks. Now Roma lives in a home for such children in North Shropshire, where Margaret and I have twice been to see her. It is most humanely run – she could not, I think, be in

better hands. And she seems content. But her life, as far as
one can judge, is that of a vegetable.

Roma died very soon after. Some readers have assumed that *A
Child Possessed* was the result of this experience. Yet in fact Roma was
born in 1968, four years *after* the publication of *A Child Possessed*. It
was a matter of life imitating art, not the other way round.

Stepan's relationship with Eugénie goes through an ever-deepening
acceptance of her inner human characteristics. He watches her being
seen by others as a 'vegetable', a 'performing dog' – he angrily rebukes
those who only see her as an interesting grotesque, a 'circus animal'
or a 'carnival effigy'. He sees her as a human who simply has 'a lot to
learn' and has his own way of interpreting her physical actions and
sounds as her own language which he needs to learn. There are many
moving descriptions of these moments when he feels he has reached
real communication with her:

> The world she lived in was remote from his: in hers, he was
> perhaps no more than a piece of shifting scenery, scarcely
> to be identified, a thing which now and then obscured
> the sun. But she was a creature who saw and heard, who
> swallowed food with evident relish, moved her body from
> one spot to another of her own choosing; however small her
> field of consciousness it must be one that fitted together.
> To enter that microcosm he needed to see with her eyes,
> to feel with her feelings; and if that leap were possible at all
> the point of departure would be some portion of his own
> experience.

He eventually feels he has reached this point, as he pulled the lorry
off the road and halted:

> As cautiously as a ploughboy set to dance with royalty he
> took her hands in his; facing her, he laughed once more,
> and when she gave the same response [deliberate squawks
> and a then an expiring hiss] he rewarded her with a smile
> through which he tried to make his gladness leap the gap
> between his eyes and hers. At one moment he thought he
> had succeeded: it appeared to him that from a point in those
> stagnant, curded orbs there shone, as a wet stone answers

moonlight, a gleam of understanding. That prodigy he knew, could have sprung from his own hopefulness, and the phase of elation was followed by a fresh despondency. But after he had released her hands they continued to rest in his, it seemed to give her pleasure when he bent and touched her fingers with his tongue, and this inspired him to try a further appeal. He made a sucking kiss in the air, he winked and laughed at her with loving eyes, and then, parting his lips and emphatically shaping the syllables with teeth and tongue, he pronounced the word 'Géniuska' several times over. The performance won her attention – for half a minute or more her head kept still. But that was not all. Her blubber lips had begun to work as if a thread were drawn inside them; suddenly she stretched her good right hand to pull at the neck of his vest, and simultaneously there came from the contorted mouth the sound 'Ka', distinctly formed and now laboriously repeated, 'Ka... Ka!' – as if she was teaching herself some lesson. The effect on him was almost overwhelming. He no longer doubted that she recognised him as a person ... He found his vision hazed by tears, his hands and his chin trembling. Some moments passed before he was enough in his own control to uncouple her harness and take her on his knees, to whisper, laughing and weeping with his forehead in her hair, 'Génie, – Géniuska – you and I, at last we know each other!'

The novel ends with Stepan desperately separated from Eugénie by a violent snowstorm. She is in Marseilles, struck down by fever, being looked after by the nervous but deeply concerned Hélène. Stepan arrives to hear that Eugénie's last sounds seemed to be an imitation of his laugh. He takes this as comfort in his grief, as he declares that he does not know how he can live without her. His moving epitaph for her is: 'He could no longer face the thought of setting out on the long haul to Lyon or Toulouse with an empty seat beside him, of climbing the tortuous stairway at the Rue des Fouines to an empty room.'

The novel was chosen for the W.H. Smith award (£1,000) for 'the most outstanding contribution to literature during the two years preceding the year of the award'. The ceremony was held in London at the Savoy Hotel, and the presentation was made by the Minister for the

Arts, Jennie Lee. The judges were Lady Huntingdon, Sir Rupert Hart-Davis, and Raymond Mortimer. On this occasion, R.C.H. attended the award ceremony and gave a reply to Rupert Hart-Davis' official presentation speech. It is a novel which has captured the imagination of many readers as their 'introduction' to the work of R.C.H. The work certainly won the attention of the novelist Sebastian Faulks and it was this novel he was referring to, describing it as: 'A humane novel on the grand scale by a mid-century English master of the genre. It asks to be compared to Balzac or Tolstoy, and is not embarrassed by the comparison.' A fellow novelist, Peter Hobbs, described it as 'certainly one the great British novels of the twentieth century, beautifully written, and is perhaps the most moral – though certainly not moralising – book I know'. Arthur Calder-Marshall wrote in the *Financial Times* that *A Child Possessed* came from the pen of 'the most underrated novelist of our time … He disregards fashion. He refuses to repeat in each book the success of others. His novels are adventures into the wilderness of the spirit where the going is rough and even paths blazed in the past are overgrown with secondary scrub.' R.C.H. would have been equally pleased to receive a letter from the managers of Ravenswood Village Settlement for Mentally Handicapped Young People, which said that they had bought a copy of the novel 'with a view to our staff using it as a text-book, and to help them understand the relationship between patients and handicapped children'.

The statement which pinpoints the essence of the novel is Stepan's declaration: 'Of this creature I know nothing certainly except that she suffers pain and fear as I do. That is enough to show she is of my kind. Her title to my devotion is simply that she suffers.' This 'sad insistent tune' resonates like the unheard, but reported final laugh of Eugénie, which lingers on the ears of some readers long after the final pages have been closed … for some, for months after … for some, for years … and for some, for life.

Chapter 7

R.C.H. and Religion

It was a plastic head, a head with a bearded face.

'Belgy! Belgy! Look what I've found! ... I think it's a Christ's head ... the statue must be somewhere. I thought if we could find it I might try to fix it on again ...'

'Why?'

'If it's Christ's head it's holy. It's God's. He made the whole world!'

The head lay with its face upwards. The Belgian raised one foot and brought the heel of his foot down on the face, crushing it to powder.

'Tell him,' he said, 'to make another world. Tell him we're dissatisfied with this one!'

The angry voice and violent foot was that of Vincent Levesque, the character looking for *The Image of My Father*. The quotation pinpoints the fact that, though R.C.H. was clearly motivated by Christian questions and beliefs throughout his life, he was no simplistic Christian propagandist. He was too much of an objective artist to allow his characters to become puppets manoeuvred into some contrived allegory. His motivation was to enter into the consciousness of individual troubled minds, and as realistically as possible see them embarking on a potential path leading towards a resolution of their suffering. His skill lay in opening spiritual doors, without entering across the threshold. This is well illustrated in the notes he made when planning the final denouement for the central character of his final novel, *Rising* (of which more later). In his *own* mind R.C.H. knows his own answer and writes in his notes:

> Only when he [Sabino] has realised that if ... like the German monks, he puts himself into the hands of the Risen Christ as His follower, he may do wrong again, he may even be proud and cruel again, but never again will he be without the knowledge that, in his new life, he can be forgiven and can find peace.

But the book is entitled *Rising*, not 'Risen' and he suggests in his notes three possible ways in which the character could confront his problems – none leading to some completed resolution, but each offering a stepping stone towards it. It is a clear indication of R.C.H.'s ability to divorce himself from his characters: he hopes that Sabino will find release from his spiritual torments but Hutchinson, like the reader, cannot see whether Sabino's future will result in any certain resolution.

The Christian element in R.C.H.'s novels is thus always implicit, rather than explicit. He fills his pages as often with plausible atheists or agnostics as with priests, monks, or missionaries. This objectivity is succinctly expressed by Virginia in *Interim*. When referring to her father's treatment of her sick mother she observes:

> I don't know if Father realizes. You'd think he must, being a doctor. And yet I don't know – doctors suffer more than anyone else from *idées fixes* about illnesses. He made up his mind when this trouble began that it was 'of nervous origin' ... and he half thinks it still is. Or doesn't he? You can't tell with these people who think about God all the time, they live in a country of their own.

R.C.H.'s own churchmanship was predictably conventional. Having run scared of the extremes of the evangelicalism of his youth, and having retreated from his brief flirtation with the Anglo-Catholicism of his step-brother, Sheldon, he adopted a middle-of-the-way Anglicanism. He was a regular communicant at his parish churches, and took his family to church each Sunday. His children, when young, remember going into their parents' bedroom and seeing them kneeling at the bedside in prayer. He did not wear his faith on his sleeve, preferring to work in the background – being church treasurer, happy to read a lesson, acting as churchwarden, but never entering the pulpit either in life or as an author. Margaret became a leading figure in the local Mothers' Union. One wonders whether he and Margaret ever remembered a letter which Margaret wrote to R.C.H. when they were engaged, and she was in Oxford and he was in Norwich, in 1927: 'Norwich will make us sleepy and respectable ... I can't see you a churchwarden or me as a president of the Mothers' Union, somehow – anyway, not for thirty or forty years!' Thirty years later that was exactly what they had become!

R.C.H.'s daughter, Elspeth, remembers as a child of about 7 or 8 attending church when her father was reading the lesson. It was not long after the publication of *Testament*. She assumed, with pride, that R.C.H. was reading from his own book.

R.C.H. only wrote three articles of any length about his own thoughts of the experience of being a writer. In one of them, 'My Apologia', published in *John O'London's Weekly* in 1949 (and reissued five months later in *The Saturday Review of Literature* as 'If One Must Write Fiction ...') he considers what he sees as the 'moral' stance of being a writer – a profession which he declares to be:

> of the several occupations I have tried ... very much the hardest, the loneliest, the most exasperating. I frequently think that it is also the most selfish. The priest and the ploughman are necessary to mankind. Those who make soap or sell bicycles perform services which justify their existence. Even the story-teller, if he sticks to romance or detection, fulfils a need of human society. But it is not evident that the novelist who spends all his time trying to satisfy what he calls his artistic conscience is fulfilling any such need. Further, I fancy that if such a novelist tries to ease his moral conscience by deliberately introducing a didactic element into his work he generally courts disaster: the control which he exercises upon his characters derives from certain intuitions and if, forsaking those intuitions, he uses characters as instruments for teaching moral lessons, they will die. Moral passion, taken at boiling point, may produce work which has both moral and artistic value. Fiction derived from a calculated morality will have neither.

> That statement, however, I believe to be incomplete …
> The fundamental concern of the fictionist is to represent
> truth as he perceives it, with the greatest possible fidelity;
> on that fidelity the artistic value of his work depends, and
> it would at least be difficult to argue that this concern has
> no relation to morality. Shortly, I believe, that in so far as
> he succeeds in the artistic purpose of illuminating an area
> of truth – the actualities of human nature – the novelist
> performs a unique function which cannot be without moral
> value.

He continues, with words which capture, in a nutshell, the thoughts
behind the novels he was about to embark on, which have been
discussed in the previous chapters:

> I can only suggest that a certain absence of stature which has
> been observed in much contemporary fiction may be due
> to the mechanistic conception of human character which
> now widely prevails; for if the human being is considered
> merely as the resultant of heredity, environment, definable
> complexes, then the description of his mental and physical
> behaviour comes to have only the interest which attaches
> to problems in mathematics. The splendour possible in
> fiction will never come, I think, except from discovering
> in every human (good or bad, intelligent or idiotic) a value
> far higher than that which he derives from having, in the
> last few hundred millennia, come to surpass the lower
> animals in sentience and understanding: an individual
> and unique value, acquired from an extra-natural force.
> I fancy that the *raison d'être* of a novelist is to be found
> in that conception, which is fundamental to his business;
> and also, as I understand it, fundamental in the Christian
> philosophy.

Perhaps he was expressing this view in the words of the narrator
in a short story ('The Last Page'): 'I realise more then, more strongly
than ever before, the tragedy of a well-developed moral sense in a
religious agnostic.'

In his acceptance speech for the award for *A Child Possessed*, he
summarised his view in simple terms: '[A] novel only comes to its full

stature when it defies every determinist philosophy, when it *accepts* the mysterious, the numinous, when it recognizes in every human being not only a marvellous machinery but also a unique and divine creation.'

In even more succinct terms, he stated his convictions in a private letter to a clerical friend and used the telling phrase which pinpoints the source of his artistic concern in the majority of his post-war novels: 'the mystery of pain':

> I try within the limits that fiction allows to let it reflect the Christian philosophy, as far as my knowledge of that philosophy allows; because I believe, albeit it with a very scanty theological equipment, that no other attitude towards the mystery of pain, which is the great mystery, has any value.

Chapter 8

Two Further Novels

Two novels written between 1946 and 1971, *Elephant and Castle* and *Origins of Cathleen*, refuse to fit into any general category in terms of tone and content. Yet they interestingly share some similarities and also some contrasts. They are both novels set in the British Isles – in London and in Ireland – and both use a narrator called Hutchinson. In the case of *Elephant and Castle* Hutchinson (also with the Christian name Raymond) is the main narrator (there is also a minor character called Fredrick Hutchinson); in *Origins of Cathleen* the narrator is Mr Hutchinson as an adult, but seen as a boy, Ryan, in the early part. *Elephant and Castle* is the second longest of the novels, only just a little shorter than *Testament*, and is written from a serious moral perspective; *Origins of Cathleen* is a novel of medium length and is R.C.H.'s experiment in writing an almost entirely comic novel. Both represent novels in which R.C.H. seems to be deliberately setting himself particularly demanding (though almost opposite) narrative challenges.

R.C.H. began *Elephant and Castle* in 1946 but its composition was interrupted by the writing of *Paiforce* and most of *Recollections of a Journey* before being completed in 1949. Since 1940 he had been considering a novel depicting working-class life in London and chose the district of 'The Elephant and Castle', south of the Thames, for its setting.

It is difficult not to see the shadow of Dickens behind R.C.H.'s imagination as he portrays the hustle and bustle, the sights and sounds, the cries of tradesmen, the clip-clop of horses' hooves across cobbles, and the secret and colourful lives of the inhabitants in the crowded, ramshackle houses that comprised Mickett Lane. One recalls R.C.H.'s pleasure in visiting London, described in his schoolboy diary: 'London: how it advances, how it hums. There is nothing in the world like it, with its light and traffic and shape and people.'

But it is not just the description of place that is Dickensian, there is also a similar flow of the pen in characterisation. He depicts a middle-aged woman in a court room:

> Her lips moved busily, as if in a dumb show of lecturing, her puzzled eyes went every way like a six-month baby's, but her head remained completely still, couched, a little on one side, in her rolling breast and shoulders as a chop lies in a dish of mashed potato.

And he evokes the figure of a bald proprietor of a gym for young men: 'He wore a running vest and a pair of loose serge trousers, he appeared to have been planed and finished off with emery paper, you felt he could only be entirely happy when pulling up trees.' He combines Dickensian extremes of humour and tenderness – there is a farcical car chase at a wedding and favourite Hutchinson comedy of moving furniture; these are shared with poignant death scenes and a description of child birth.

The cast list is also Dickensian in scope – some 90 names appear in the list of characters, augmented by: 'Boys at Apostles' Court; members of the Belgrave Bradlaugh Society and other free philosophers; residents in Weald Street and Mickett Lane; Priests and Nuns; workmen, shopkeepers, drivers, porters, policemen, gaolers; a Prison Chaplain; a press-photographer; and some others.'

The biographer has to admit to a serious and mystifying problem at this point. Many readers of the novels will constantly detect the ghost of Dickens, and never more so than in *Elephant and Castle*. One also recalls R.C.H.'s schoolboy pleasure in hearing Dickens being recited. Furthermore, R.C.H. writes with enthusiasm of seeing Emlyn Williams in a one-man show as Dickens. All this suggests a life-long intimate knowledge of Dickens on R.C.H.'s part. Yet one has to refer to a letter written to Martyn Skinner in 1970 which includes the words: 'By the way, I am a non-Dickensian. Never read the chap. Always meant to.' Yet in a later letter (cited in Chapter 2) he makes a specific reference to Dickens' description of a horse being given 'a shrewd cuff' across the buttocks in R.C.H.'s own description of his efforts to ride a horse. In a short story, R.C.H. has a character looking at a shelf of books: 'There was a whole row of Balzac, but oddly enough ... as far as I could see, no Dickens.' The interesting phrase is 'oddly enough'. The biographer must simply record that, though Dickens seems to be a regular and lively literary influence, the author claims – mysteriously – never to have read him.

The plot of *Elephant and Castle* moves along three main avenues: the evocation of London, the unhappy relationship between a working-class man and his middle-class, patronising wife, and the story of a murder which is being unravelled throughout the book – another Dickensian echo from *The Mystery of Edwin Drood*, perhaps. The marriage and the murder are inextricably connected, for Gian is the suspected murderer and Armorel is his wife. The origin of the story appears in a notebook of R.C.H.'s of 1940: 'Girl who "reclaims" criminal and marries him. Criminal does not respond. Gradually revealed that criminal has the real virtues, honesty etc., while girl is really moral poseuse.'

Gian is uneducated, quick to descend to outbursts of violent temper, an ex-prisoner who lives in a world inhabited by guns and knives. But he has the ability to see beneath the surface of his fellow beings, unlike Armorel who sees Gian as a 'challenge', a character to be nurtured and civilised by intelligent guidance but is – in the words of a character who knows her well – 'utterly selfish and viciously cruel'. Another perceptive character tells her: 'You think you're being kind to him, and what you're really doing is giving him a special kind of hell.'

The sleight of hand with which R.C.H. is able to fuse two strands of the novel together is well illustrated by the memories of the narrator (Raymond) describing a scene in a court during a trial attempting to discover the facts about the murder. It recalls the evidence given by a lodger in Gian's home – an unkempt character, leaning awkwardly over the witness bar. It evokes both the shambolic world of Mickett Lane, but also the heart of generosity which lies beneath the squalor – in contrast to the superficial world of 'respectability' lived in by those who do not recognise such a possibility existing in such a 'thoroughfare':

> His self-contradictions seemed to be symbolic of the conflict
> of human purposes, his sprawling body and recalcitrant

clothes a demonstration of men's non-conformity with the tidy process of formal reasoning. Here, in place of the 'thoroughfare to which m'learned friend has referred' was Mickett Lane itself, rancid and seedy but exhaling a warm breath, betraying through chinks in its commonplace exterior a huge entanglement of vital privacies. Those others, I thought at the time, represent the mechanics of morality, working smoothly enough. This decrepit creature reminds us of what morality is about.

The novel's subtitle is 'A Reconstruction' and the novel is thus not just an imaginative reconstruction of London, and an imaginative reconstruction of a murder in the 1930s in Mickett Lane, but the difficulties of reconstructing this accurately. Such ambiguities underlie everything in the book, as seen through the eyes of a sceptical narrator. The novel opens with a statement of the unreliability of establishing objective truth:

> The facts will be stated and you shall make your own judgements. In the strictest sense, it is impossible to give facts uncoloured by opinion. When a man says 'We had dirty weather' you know that he disliked it; another would have said 'It was fresh and exhilarating, though there was a good deal of rain.' No one can relate all the circumstances, and those which a man selects, deliberately or not, will owe their inclusion at least a little to his prejudices, as well as to his habits in observation and memory. But remember, too, that your own prejudices operate all the time. Whatever comes to your mind comes through your own screen of intricate associations: the memory of something said in a schoolmaster's sarcastic voice; the loneliness of a foreign city; a soldier's kindness in a railway carriage when the first light was revealing frosted fields; defections and disillusionments. The phrase 'What I should have done ...' marks, as a rule, a misunderstanding of the nature of things. The largest mistake about truth is to imagine that it is simple.

Later, another narrator sees Raymond Hutchinson sorting through his mass of family archives: 'Somewhere among all these documents one must discover truth and reality. So Raymond thought.'

But if the novel mirrors the tone of a typical nineteenth-century novel, it ends quite differently with an excursion into two pages of internal monologue and 'stream of consciousness', as Gian faces the dawn of an apparent execution day, with a moving mixture of confusion and resolute bravery at the last:

> Got to think. Just a bit o' time, bit more time to think. Might see how it work, just a bit more time. 'Loves you.' Same as me lovin Sue an' Tonie. Dark. Gone all dark. 'Wait! I got something to say! Wait! *Wait!* Let me go, let go my arms, let me get out. *I got something to say! Got something to say! Let me out!'* They can't do that. Sort of a joke. Dream. Sort of a joke. Not really. Won't happen. Somethin' go wrong. Won't really happen … Jes's Chris'. Jes's Chris'. Jes's Chris'. Love me. Sake amen. Now. Stop them. Don't let them! *Let me out!* Love me. Jes's Chris'. Jes's Chris'…. Terror, naked, the endless moment of terror like sky splitting, like a sword of ice driven upward from the bowels to throat. Pain like mountains falling together upon one small creature. *Love me – Jes' Chris'!* The terror and the pain, the pain and the darkness, darkness and peace. The peace, the Peace.

The novel was acclaimed in the United States, where it was first published (perhaps aided by R.C.H. making a pre-publication publicity tour to New York) and it made the best-sellers list in the United Kingdom a few months later. The critics were, as usual, mixed in their opinions, with Philip Toynbee being predictably acerbic, declaring that R.C.H. would not survive as a novelist because he has not 'contributed to our inheritance' and found *Elephant and Castle* 'peculiarly displeasing. Mr. Hutchinson writes with a lush flamboyance which cloys and sickens.' Some found it overlong, but R.C.H. would have been encouraged by Elizabeth Bowen's observation that it needed to be long because 'its action covers nearly twenty years, its theme is formidable and its exploration of the soul requires space'. Even more pleasing were Stevie Smith's words: 'This novel touches the heights and depths of human conduct and motive. Absolutely first-rate.'

The idea for *Origins of Cathleen* are recorded in a note-book entry of 1962: '(? next novel. English family. Fairly comic but profound. Autobiographical – perhaps written as if it were my own autobiography. Amused but affectionate.)' The emphasis is on the fact that it is *not* an actual autobiography but is an imaginative idea of what such a work might be. Ryan's birthday in the novel is within months of R.C.H.'s own; Ryan's father, Howard, is Irish by descent. R.C.H.'s Irish heritage came from his mother, while Ryan's mother is Russian. Further insight comes from the draft of a letter to R.C.H.'s publisher, Michael Joseph, some ten years later:

> Perhaps every writer lives in fear of getting into a rut – of delivering, in ideas or in style, the mixture as before. When I finished *Johanna At Daybreak*, a sombre story, I felt the need to write in an entirely different mood. There is in *Origins of Cathleen* a serious theme, centred on a young Irishman whose general behaviour conceals a deep perplexity; but the story is presented mainly as comedy. I discovered the comedy I needed by exploring, with elderly eyes, a small boy of ludicrous fancies and appalling self-esteem: it was helpful to find myself strangely, disquietingly familiar with the mental processes of that insufferable child. He has portrayed himself with only a little professional guidance from me.

Origins of Cathleen is R.C.H.'s exploration into the inner mind of a growing child. It is appropriate that he dedicated it 'For all my Grandchildren'.

The novel opens with the arrival of a new governess for Ryan's sister, Anastasia – who seldom has a governess who survives many months. She is a German widow, Helma O'Kneale. Ryan, aged 11, is convinced that she is a German spy and turns himself into a secret agent to expose her. Helma also has an infant daughter, Cathleen, for whom Ryan develops a growing affection. The Hutchinson family are presented as completely chaotic, consisting of strong personalities all of whom live in absurdly imaginative and obsessive worlds.

The humour is presented in a variety of quick characterisations and some extended comic set-pieces. Mervyn Horder, in his article on R.C.H. in the *London Magazine*, draws attention to descriptions in *Origins of Cathleen* which are examples of what he calls R.C.H.'s ability to conjure a 'cascade of outrageous imagery':

> Like a sausage fried too fast her wooden face was split transversely by a monstrous smile.

> Elisabet heaved her tremendous body on to her short but sturdy legs, letting her other offspring cling or fall as their strength allowed, like commuters in a suburban train. [She is a prize sow.]

The second part of the novel moves to Ireland and allows R.C.H. to pay homage with his Irish origins. It is a reminiscence of Howard's decision to take the 7-year-old Ryan to visit his dying grandfather, and consists of a series of farcical episodes evoking typical Irish extravagant humour. The first involves the grandfather insisting on saying farewell to his favourite cow, Janet Aruba. Instead of furniture being moved, this involves getting the animal upstairs to the patient's bedroom. She seems anxious to say farewell and leans over the bed to lick her owner's face. Alarmed, one visitor – the 'General' – who is never without his Mauser, prepares to shoot her, though the gun fails to fire.

A further comic set-piece consists of describing an annual memorial to a local hero who was murdered by the English in 1835. It takes place by 'Rory's Oak' – where the hero was hiding before being shot. A bizarre procession follows, led by a top-hatted, frock-coated village dignitary (but without collar or tie) being pulled in a dilapidated wagon drawn by two emaciated donkeys. A decision to dignify proceedings by approaching the site by water involved a derelict ferry boat being erratically pulled by rebellious children in their Sunday best.

Some time later, Ryan is taken back to the river, where there is a celebration of the 'Day of the Singing Water' when a travelling, exhausted preacher bravely carried a gnarled old woman across the turbulent river. He sings as he strides across the water and the waters join in his melody. Reaching the shore, the old woman is turned into a beautiful young lady. This remarkable event is recelebrated months later in Totteridge, North London, at a riverside picnic. The old song is sung (St Dirwyn's Anthem) again to a tune remarkably resembling that of 'Hark the Herald Angels Sing':

> Hausted high a-brole the water,
>   Ah day, brach day, rankin-ho ...

A final autobiographical joke is encompassed in a conversation between Ryan and Kevin, when Kevin asks:

> And you, Ryan, do you yet know what sort of work you
> mean to do when your education is finally disposed of?
>   'I shan't go in for work', I answered easily – for I had
> given some thought to this matter. 'I'm going to write
> books instead.'

Ryan remembers that 'on a child's inexpert ear this simple prothalamium
fell with a singular charm'.

But as R.C.H. had indicated in his early notes, despite all the farce
within the novel, there is a 'serious theme' which gradually develops
as the story develops and Cathleen's origins are revealed. Linked
with this is the story of Kevin's wartime experience, and R.C.H.
returns to the moral problems of cowardice and desertion and
their consequences, which we have encountered in *The Unforgotten
Prisoner* and *The Shining Scabbard*. Although R.C.H.'s friendship
with Ernest Raymond did not begin until after the publication of the
earlier novels, one wonders whether R.C.H. may have been influenced
by the novel set in Gallipoli, *The Secret Battle*, by A.P. Herbert (like
Ernest Raymond, A.P. Herbert was a veteran of Gallipoli). R.C.H. had
earlier received a letter from A.P. Herbert admiring his work. *The
Secret Battle* tells the story of Harry Penrose, who was executed for
cowardice. The novel ends with the assertion: 'My friend Harry was
shot for cowardice – and he was one of the bravest men I ever knew.'
Kevin, in *Origins of Cathleen*, opts for a court martial, refusing to
continue to kill. Warned of the inevitable outcome, he is asked if he
is determined to proceed – 'to die disgracefully'. He replies: 'There's
different sorts of disgrace, Sir. I know my own mind on that matter.'

Richard Church described the novel as portraying a 'procession
of oddities and clowns' who turn out to be 'the human wolf-pack
gleefully escorting a saint to his execution'. The novel was turned
down by six American publishers, and has never been in print there.
The work was much more favourably received in the United Kingdom
and especially in Europe – particularly in Italy and Germany.

R.C.H. subtitled it 'A Diversion' and that is exactly how he saw it.
He had achieved an ambition to sustain a mainly humorous narrative;
now, he wrote: 'I am in the planning stage of a novel, with a theme that
seems to me important, which has been germinating for some time
past; a book which will probably take me two or three years to write.'

St Katharine's Church, Merstham where R.C.H. was churchwarden.

Margaret (left) with members of The Mothers' Union.

'I can't see you as a churchwarden or me as president of The Mothers' Union somehow, anyway, not for thirty or forty years!'
- Letter from Margaret to R.C.H. in 1927

Chapter 9

Drama and Short Stories

R.C.H. had been attracted to the theatre since childhood and always hoped that he might have some success as a dramatist. At least nine plays (written over 24 years) exist in manuscript or typescript but never got further than the study shelf. The same fate was suffered by a short radio drama. The only play that actually reached the stage was *Last Train South*. It was something of a by-product of *Testament* and is similarly concerned with the Bolshevik revolution, (*Testament* was published just three days after the last performance.) It is set (appropriately for R.C.H.) in the stationmaster's office at Pavlograd, South Russia, and covers twelve hours in the winter of 1919-20. It opened in London in August 1938 at St Martin's Theatre, Haymarket. The play had all the possibilities of success – it was directed by Basil Dean, still enjoying considerable popularity – with J.B. Priestley as co-producer. The star of the show was Flora Robson. But the play was doomed to failure and had a run of just three weeks.

The play was generally panned by the critics, most of whom blamed the production rather than the script. Basil Dean was renowned as a ruthless bully on stage and was commonly referred to by his actors as 'Bloody Basil', 'The Basilisk', and 'Bastard Basil'. He favoured extravagant theatrical effects and *Last Train South* certainly suffered from such treatment. The *News Chronicle* suggested that Dean seemed to be reaching a kind of 'second childishness' which 'mistakes noise for drama', and transformed any meaning in the play to a 'blurred meaninglessness, by a bustle of purposeless action'. Several members of the cast wrote to R.C.H. sympathising with him about the hostile reviews and blaming Dean for its critical reception. Dean also altered parts of the text just before the first performance, blurring R.C.H.'s intentions. Flora Robson wrote blaming herself for 'sitting quietly for so long'. Some have suggested that unforeseen events added to the problems, since the action took place in a bitterly cold Russian winter but was performed in the middle of a severe heat-wave in London.

There were, however, some problems in terms of narrative structure. The natural skills which enabled R.C.H. to relax on the wide stage of the novel, with slow development of character, with attention to detail in descriptions creating specific and appropriate atmosphere, are not easily transferred to the narrow stage of the theatre where compression is everything, where quick visual impact is a priority and where characterisation needs to be revealed at speed through dialogue. These problems are evident in *Last Train South*, and made the final act (with Dean's unhelpful intervention) close to producing a contrived moment of spiritual awareness – all that he had rejected in his published thoughts on the moral stance of the novelist. Alan Bott's perceptive review in the *Tatler* pin-pointed this: 'Mr. Hutchinson is an unusually good novelist; but contrasts in manner, and evocative descriptions...that usually blend in a book of 100,000 words cannot be compressed in 15,000 words of dialogue for living characters.'

Perhaps R.C.H. was aware of this. It is interesting that his type-scripts of dramas are often written under pseudonyms: Ramon Barros, Franz Wien, Francis Fielding, and Coryton Ray – as though he was hesitant to be too closely associated with the scripts.

He received letters of encouragement from J.B. Priestley – 'I believe you have a real talent and feeling for the theatre, and I hope this experience will not keep you out of it' – and from his old Oxford friend, Harold Hobson, who hoped R.C.H. would continue to write for the theatre. Flora Robson suggested that he send his next play to the director, Tyrone Guthrie. But there was to be no 'next play', and *Last Train South* joined the other dozen or so plays, unpublished and unperformed.

There was some success for an adaptation for the stage of *The Stepmother*. The somewhat eccentric script was written by Warren Chetham-Strode and the play had a well-received provincial tour before transferring to St Martin's Theatre for a month in 1958, almost exactly 20 years after the production of *Last Train South* at the same theatre. It had a warm reception, and the character of Vere attracted most interest – partly because the part was played by Maggie Smith, a performance acclaimed by Doris Lessing. After London, it had several productions by repertory companies, mostly in the south of England. It remained the only successful adaptation of a Hutchinson novel. Neil Paterson wrote a film script of *The Stepmother* for Paramount and Guy Green produced a screenplay *Stephen's Child* based on *A Child Possessed*, but like the two adaptations of *March the Ninth* already mentioned, they never reached the screen.

It is a different picture when we turn to R.C.H. as a writer of short stories (he was an admirer of Saki), which he published successfully throughout his life. Indeed, his first entry into print was a short story 'Every Twenty Years', written when he was at Oxford and published in 1928. He received £7 from the *Empire Review* and a further £2 from Jonathan Cape for its inclusion in an anthology, bringing his total earnings for his first year as a published writer to £9. His final short story appeared 37 years later in 1965.

At the time of his death, he had published 28 stories and left a further 26 unpublished ones. They appeared in a variety of magazines and journals – *English Review, The Saturday Book, The Evening News* – and also, on three occasions, he read a new one on radio for the BBC National Programme. After R.C.H.'s death, Robert Green compiled a collection entitled *The Quixotes*, and selected 26 stories, omitting six published ones and adding four unpublished ones. They vary in length between three pages and fourteen and, surprisingly, R.C.H. seems at home in the miniature world of the story, achieving sharp atmospheric atmosphere and believable characterisation through swift strokes of the pen. The subject matter covers familiar territory – war, (especially war memories) – and repeatedly the settings involve modes of transport: trains, cars, buses, boats. The difference from the novels is the emphasis on the supernatural, on dreams (usually nightmares) and apparently ghostly influences, resulting from alarming coincidences – the buses and trains are threateningly empty, their destination uncertain and uncontrollable. The stories often move to a striking and unexpected final sentence.

Several of these motifs (war, dreams, and ghosts) are evident in a typically atmospheric opening in the first paragraph of *The Last Page*:

> In February 1922 I was in Ypres ... the memory of which
> is fixed for ever in my mind as that of ruin, uncanny
> desertion, and bleak discomfort, the ghost of a town that

had been … the town which I still think of as belonging to a horrible dream.

R.C.H. would have been pleased that the volume had the title *The Quixotes*, evoking one of his favourite authors from childhood. It is also the title of one of the stories, and an extract from it might stand as a description of R.C.H.'s imaginative stance within the bounds of the short story:

> It was Bill's fault … Bill's ridiculous quixotism – it was the quixotes who were at the bottom of half the trouble in this world. But wasn't he a Quixote, in his own way? 'Disregard your own feelings. Obey the dictates of duty.' That was a fine motto, his motto, fine and Spartan and impracticable; the very badge of quixotism. Damn it, was there any sense in things at all? Could you ever get away from the cross-currents of emotionalism?

One story made an unusual impact beyond the usual territory of the average short story reader, 'Excursion to Norway'. Its origins stemmed from a request from the British Information Services that R.C.H. write something about the war to honour the bravery of the men who had fought. The result was a short account of an actual action against Vaagso in December 1940. It was published in *Atlantic Monthly*. The editor, Edward Weekes, wrote to the Ministry of Information that it was: 'The very narrative I have been hungering for for months. The intricacy of the raid, the character of the men who undertook it and the authenticity of what they did, have all been set down without a shadow of doubt. It is a brilliant piece of writing.'

It is thus different in tone to any of the other stories, being based on fact. It is a vivid account of an action of which R.C.H. had no personal knowledge, but it has none of the diverting qualities exhibiting his skill in creating an entirely fanciful narrative. He was paid $250 on its publication – the only time he was paid for what amounted to propaganda.

Perhaps the most striking story was a previously unpublished one, written in R.C.H.'s Norwich days, 'The Wall Not Made with Hands'. It describes the life of a married couple who live in a house with a room with two doors at opposite ends. Each of them always enters and leaves through their own door. They act as though there is a glass wall dividing the room so neither can cross to the other half. They communicate through the glass, and express themselves by hand signals pressed against the partition. This causes confusion to a visitor who witnesses their strange way of making contact without actually doing so. They tell him that the wall has been there ever since they married. But when he speaks to them individually they each admit that they only play their individual roles because the other believes the wall to exist. The visitor leaves pondering the problem of which of the two believes what, or whether both are living in a fantasy world – but a world which makes them both happy. It is a moving description of a relationship based on mutual understanding – or shared delusion.

Not surprisingly, the stories are set in a variety of geographical locations – France, the Middle East, Scandinavia. His final excursion into this literary form was 'Anniversary', set in South America, dealing with the contradictory moralities and loyalties and political beliefs of opposing factions of a revolution: a whole novel compressed into nine pages. It appeared in 1965, six years before R.C.H. began working on his final literary challenge and ten years before this challenge was published. 'Anniversary' can thus be seen as a kind of first sketch for what was to become his farewell to the world of fiction: *Rising*.

Chapter 10

Last Days and *Rising*

From the mid-1960s, domestic life for R.C.H. became more relaxed. He was happy in Bletchingley playing the part of welcoming grandfather (there were nine grandchildren by 1970), spending more time tending the garden and performing duties at his chosen parish church, St Katharine's, Merstham. He also enjoyed visits to the theatre – The Mermaid in London to see his old friend Maurice Denham on stage, and attending local venues: a new theatre in Leatherhead, a reopened theatre in East Grinstead, together with the Theatre Royal in Brighton, and the Ashcroft Theatre in Croydon. He also took pleasure in the opera, with performances at Croydon and particularly in visits to Glyndebourne.

But there were customary contradictions in lifestyle as he began to travel more, now that he was reaching the end of his imaginative literary journeys, with expeditions to Sardinia, Palermo, Calabria, and Rome. He developed an affection for southern France and visited Ireland and Margaret's family connections in western Scotland. He was increasingly writing letters to appreciative readers and friends – his correspondence with Martyn Skinner becoming frequent and lengthy, and often showing a relaxed humour:

> Perhaps I've told you of the churchwarden in a Kentish church whom I saw going up to read the First Lesson with his open jacket displaying miles of Old Harrovian tie. He read from *Genesis*: And Jacob said to them, 'Whence come ye?' And they said, 'From Harrar.' I quivered with

excitement, expecting the next words to be 'By Jove – I come from Harrar too.'

And in another letter:

> It is of course a well-known diagnostic of senility, this failure to realize the passage of time. I was sharply reminded of this last week when I bought a working jacket in a cheap-john shop in Croydon. The salesman, reading my name stamped on the back of my cheque, said: 'R.C. Hutchinson – there used to be an author called that.' I left him to his gentle memories.

But it was not just to be a life a cultural evenings, enjoyable touring, and musing among the roses and delphiniums in the garden, for he had for some time had a project in his mind – another wide-ranging novel which he felt would be a challenging literary finale.

It is always tempting to a biographer to find convenient pigeonholes to order a writer's life, which can sometimes be more misleading than enlightening, but in R.C.H.'s case it does seem as though his final novel is in many ways a mature rewriting of his first novel which he dismissed as 'balderdash'. He was imagining a foreign landscape, a country in revolution, a world of corruption in both economic and political terms, with a principal character deeply troubled emotionally and romantically, and the whole scenario under the spell of an enigmatic faith healer who may or may not have survived intense torture. The difference between *Thou Hast A Devil* and *Rising* is that the tone and characterisation have moved from the mostly more simple first-person narrative and two-dimensional individuals to a deeper and broader poetic vision and more rounded and psychologically complicated personalities. In 1971 he was still struggling with the demands of narrative:

> Broadly, the snag about first-person narrative is that, as soon as you introduce dialogue (which the reader demands) you imply 'total recall', which is absurd; but when you narrate in the third-person, giving yourself liberty to enter every character's mind, you are pretending to be God; which in my case is equally absurd! Having said that, I do agree that to ask the reader to believe that an elderly man remembers

long speeches made to him when he was seven is carrying
the first-person convention fantastically far.

What differentiates the writing of *Rising* from all the other novels is
that, having decided on the setting, R.C.H. travelled to South America with Margaret to base the writing on first-hand knowledge rather
than secondary research. Hence, in March 1971, he set off on a 17,000-
mile journey through Venezuela, Argentina, Chile, Bolivia, and five
further countries. The novel is thus full of authentic descriptions
of flora and fauna, of varied weather changes, vivid portrayals of
scenery and many contrasting conditions of social and economic
living conditions. He also engaged in careful historical background,
reading Che Guevera's *Bolivian Diary*, Mao Tse-Tung's On *Guerrilla
Warfare*, Fawcett's explorations of South America, and Prescott's
history of the conquest of Mexico, together with Blakemore's *Latin
America*.

In the same way that we have no evidence of R.C.H. having read
Dickens, we have a similar lack of evidence of his having read the
novelist with whom many critics and readers feel he had close affinities:
Joseph Conrad. It was in 1904 that Conrad published *Nostromo*, set
in an imaginary South American country – and *Rising* opens in 1903.
The parallels between the two novels are striking. *Nostromo* centres
on the protection of a silver mine by the incorruptible Charles Gould
and Don Pepe (reversed in *Rising* to the less than impeccable de Juanos
mining family); the upholders of morality and religion in *Nostromo*,
Father Roman and Father Corbelan, have their counterparts in
Rising in the figures of the inscrutable Bishop, and of Diego, Dona
Marta, and the German monks; the political and social uprisings of
Ribiera and Montero in *Nostromo* are mirrored in the struggles over
the railway line between Sabino and his adopted brothers in *Rising*.
Dominating everything in *Nostromo* is the charismatic figure of
Nostromo himself, whose real name is Fidanza (Trust). He is replaced
by Sabino – fanatical, arrogant, brutal, revengeful – who is seeking
vengeance on the memory of the spiritual healer and doctor, Papac,
whom he blames for the desertion of his wife and whom he left for
dead some time before. (One might add some intriguing parallel
themes with another author who shared many of R.C.H.'s views, but
for whom there is no evidence of any personal connection: Graham
Greene. *The Power And The Glory*, set in Mexico, was published
in 1940.)

It took R.C.H. four years to work on *Rising*, though he never completed the final chapter. He confided to Martyn Skinner in 1971 that he was plagued by his slowness in moving the story forward, and dealing with the complications he had set himself:

> At the moment I am all tied up with a very large list of characters. (Yes, they are supposed to live somewhere between Iquitos and Antofagasta; but somehow the scenery keeps wandering about rather. When mountains get in the way I move them a hundred kilometres east or west, hoping the reader will be too sleepy to notice), with appallingly complex thoughts and relations, lives which mean a great deal to me and with which, I fear, no publisher, let alone the 'general reader,' will have any patience.

And two years later he wrote:

> I'm making heavy weather of it. I've bitten off more than I can chew. The supposed reader has long been asleep and snoring (as I often snore myself, after trying to wrestle with one of Proust's longer and more involved and disquisitionary paragraphs). I do three or four paragraphs a day: at sixty-six, and feeling ninety, with various trivial ailments that other men sensibly ignore, I tire easily. On most days it appears to me that every word in the English Language ends in ION. On other days every word ends in NCE ... At least a third of the book – at a rough guess – is still to be done. I gravely doubt if anyone will publish it. In some inexplicable, perhaps masochistic, way I still rather *enjoy* this ridiculous activity.

The researcher is rewarded by the fact that these problems of composition resulted in R.C.H. making copious, detailed notes which chart the progress of his thoughts and dilemmas. In his notes for the 'blurb', he suggested that the novel was an 'amalgam of realism and poetic imagination'. It is this amalgam that makes any quick illustration of the novel's tone almost impossible. We are on familiar territory in some matters – there is exotic vocabulary ('a cincture of demilunes'), and we meet a deformed dwarf, Ugil, in Sabina's faithful servant. Once again, the whole novel is both a spiritual and physical journey, this time mostly on foot or horseback. Some of the slow-developing poetic pace which gave the novel what S. Kennedy in *The Times Literary Supplement* called 'a mythic proportion' in its description of 'the nightmarish journey across rivers and mountains' is evident as Sabino's son, Patricio, muses on the events of the previous day's misery:

> The loss of his identity was itself a gain; for the men he had commanded became in a sense his teachers, deeply versed in the business of suffering, and the closer his union with them the larger grew his share of their peculiar resignation. They as a body had finally accepted their engagement as one without bounds or purpose, or falling into their state of mind, was infected by their stoic self-command. Often the agony of swollen joints, a tidal weakness born of hunger and fatigue, brought him near to surrender; then he would glimpse a man called Taupir who used his single arm to press angrily upon one knee and then the other, he would get a grin from the lame Laurico or would catch from the Stygian orchestra of groans and gasping the cracked, defiant voice of an old Otuma tribesman who never ceased to sing. From such men came an illusion of invincibility: if they could march on nothing but their human valiance so could he. Some end must come. Today – he thought, when one of the sturdiest marchers had dropped on his knees and died – today must be the last: when darkness falls again it will lie on us as the coverlid of stones and soil lies now on that man's body, so heavily that no call to be up and moving will disturb us; then, without dishonour, we shall rest. But the darkness when it came was only a scarf laid fleetingly across their eyes, the perfunctory prelude to another day. Another? Or yesterday returned? Nothing had changed. Flat and empty as mid-ocean, uniform as a prison yard, the brown monotony of parched and lifeless earth ended only where it fused with the haze of the far sky. In a scene so limitless, so constant the thought of gaining ground seemed fantasy. Yet the human structure at its centre was still perceptibly advancing ... These simple beings halted at command and dropped as if the current they worked from had been disconnected, but at the shout

of *'Adelante!'* every one of them came back to life; night turned them to a cluster of discarded corpses, another day began and the ragged herd was once more on its feet: moving a shade more slowly now, trammelled by locked joints and swollen ankles, by the agony that showed in distorted mouths and famished eyes, but with a mysterious persistence, as men, who have taken the measure of eternity.

Kennedy in *The Times Literary Supplement* continues to observe R.C.H.'s skill to fuse the poetic tone with the force of realism:

> Although the confrontation with Papac, which transforms Sabino physically and spiritually, takes place in a dreamlike state, it is firmly rooted in reality. By a gloriously rich use of language (occasionally giving way to a self-conscious obscurantism), Mr. Hutchinson meticulously creates a whole society and topography.

The notebooks make clear what R.C.H.'s intentions were and the extent to which he wanted the breadth and realism of his canvas to extend. He made a list of twelve areas he needed to explore: 'Principles, Questions, Schema, Possible Names, Vocabulary, Animal Life, Vegetation, People, Odd Details, Food & Drink, Diseases, Diagram (of the Geography).'

The section 'Questions' includes eight sub-divisions, asking such questions as: 'What about the servants, farmhands, at Quinta El Duque? Are any left? Where have the rest got to? Are they likely to return?' and 'Who is to straighten out Sabino's thought/emotions? Diego or Maria? And *when*?'. Particularly interesting are two sub-sections under 'Principles':

> 7. Poetry. Nervous style, enriched by observation of the curious and beautiful. Beware of over-elaborate sentences, paragraphs.
>
> 8. Family Relationships. Somewhat Proustian. A certain lack of intimacy, perhaps, but a tired, defensive sense of holding together in a common cause – surviving (without effort), preserving their industrial empire – which the influence of Atun Papac threatens.

He also commits himself to objectivity in terms of the motives for revolution: 'It is of the first importance to delineate carefully the idea of violent revolution against that of revolution-by-love. The violent revolutionary's ideas – impatience, despair, practicality etc; etc; – must be carefully and sympathetically studied.'

R.C.H. continues:

> There are three forces in operation:
> (1) Sabino – representing power/status/wealth (roughly)
> (2) the form of revolutionary protest, headed by an intelligent, resolute, ruthless man.
> (3) The ultimately winning force of love represented by Papac (3) needs to be hinted at – planted delicately – all the way through the book. It is the one which Sabino cannot cope with because of his spiritual poverty, of which he is always vaguely aware – and for which he compensates himself by violence.

The novel was published in 1976, a year after R.C.H.'s death. Among the reviews (mixed as ever) one of the most appreciative was in *The Northern Echo*:

> The stature of this book is difficult to convey in so few words, with its multi-dimensional grasp of the power of the mind for good or ill, or of the will for bodily endurance; and its poet's apprehension of the beauties and cruelties of terrestrial wilderness, and the lapidary quality of observed detail. Though one might carp at longeurs, this is a major work from a major author.

There were of course difficulties in dealing with the problems of publishing an unfinished work. R.C.H.'s son, Jeremy, using careful analysis of the notebooks, provided a possible conclusion to the missing end of the final chapter. This was close to being accepted as a suitable solution by the publishers, Michael Joseph, but it was eventually decided to leave it in its unfinished form with a brief afterword of explanation by Margaret giving some of R.C.H.'s possible conclusions as sketched out in his notes. Like Schubert's 'Unfinished Symphony', *Rising* seemed to cause little problems to many readers – feeling that it was somehow appropriate to the whole nature of the novel's core tone. One of R.C.H.'s suggestions for a 'blurb' for the novel read:

> Ostensibly the study of an episode in South American history, it is at a deeper level an examination of racial and other human relationships, of the tragedy of alienation ... the eternal problem of evil. It hints at a key/solution/answer to the problem.

The key word is 'hints' and perhaps the unfinished nature of the novel is the most definitive power of a 'hint' to the sensitive reader.

An unexpected confusion resulted from a misprint on the dust jacket (which had also appeared on the cover of *Origins of Cathleen*) which attributed the quotation, 'R.C. Hutchinson will be read fifty – perhaps a hundred – years hence' to C.S. Lewis (with whom R.C.H. had no connection) rather than to C. Day Lewis.

On 3 July 1975, R.C.H. was working on *Rising* in his study at Bletchingley before joining Margaret for lunch with two welcome visitors – their old friend Diana Raymond and another friend, Betty McCullough. Diana had called Margaret earlier in the week saying, 'Oh, I do hope that Thursday will be gloriously fine.' They had a convivial lunch which extended to afternoon tea.

When the visitors left, R.C.H. was rather irritated by a vehicle blocking the roadway, but having waved goodbye to their guests, R.C.H. and Margaret returned indoors. R.C.H. went upstairs and Margaret was clearing the tea cups in the living room when she was disturbed by a noise upstairs. She discovered R.C.H. on the floor of the bathroom having suffered a sudden and fatal heart attack. In a typically accepting response, Margaret later phoned Diana recalling their earlier conversation saying, 'Well, Thursday was gloriously fine for *him*.' It could have been the final sentence of an R.C.H. novel.

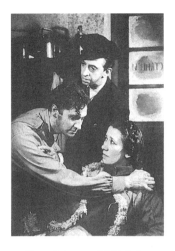

R.C.H. and Margaret, off the coast of Peru, 1971.

Peter Murray Hill, John Abbott and Flora Robson in 'Last Train South', 1938.

R.C.H. in garden at Dysart.

R.C.H. and Margaret's grave at St. Katharine's Church, Merstham.

Epilogue

As early as September 1969, R.C.H. wrote a letter to Martyn Skinner which reads as a poignantly prophetic account about the writing of *Rising*. He suggests that the novel will have a 'terrific ending', but he doubts that he will find the right words, and also doubts whether he will be able to finish the novel 'even if I survive'. How accurate his premonitions were in terms of the novel's composition! But sadly he was never to know the impact that his unfinished manuscript briefly had. In 1976, *Rising* was selected for the long-list for the Booker Prize, and Ladbroke's gave odds on the twelve 'most highly-fancied runners' with *Rising* quoted at 12-1. When it entered the short-list of five it was quoted at 4-1. (The judges were Walter Allen, Francis King and Lady Wilson – wife of the former Prime Minister, Harold Wilson – and the final winner was David Storey's *Saville*.)

At the short-list stage, it was discovered that the prize was restricted to living novelists and as R.C.H. had died before publication, *Rising* was ineligible. It was perhaps a final and appropriately incomplete ending to both the novel and R.C.H.'s authorial vision.

The funeral was held at St Katharine's Church, Merstham, and the organ was played by R.C.H.'s grandson Gregory (later to become Regius Professor of Greek at Oxford). Considering R.C.H.'s first pronouncements in his schoolboy diary of the pre-eminence of love in Christian belief, and repeating this conviction at the end of his life in his notes for the conclusion of *Rising*:

> The main thing in all this is the supremacy of love. Can one avoid using that word – is there a complete synonym? The love we are concerned with is the *Christian* love. It is the business of Diego and/or Marta to lead Sabino to

see that love as thus understood, *positive*, creative, utterly altruistic, is the solvent, the answer, the only rescue.

It was appropriate that one of the chosen hymns was 'O Love that wilt not let me go', with the telling line, 'I trace the rainbow through the rain.' R.C.H. is buried in a simple grave in St Katharine's churchyard.

So many of the novels centre on the use of and understanding of the power of participial adjectives – clear in titles such as *The Answering Glory, Shining Scabbard, One Light Burning,* and *Rising.* R.C.H. had a habit in his notebooks of using different coloured inks to represent aspects of importance or direction. Green was his chosen colour for special emphasis. It was in green that he wrote a final intention for the end of *Rising* – a fitting epitaph for R.C.H. both as novelist and person: 'We want, finally, a sense of things not ending but freshly beginning.'

His novels will always remain a rich reward for those who share, or can sympathise with, this vision – that however deep the nature of human suffering maybe, there can always be 'One Light Burning'.

Select Bibliography

A fuller bibliography can be found in *R.C. Hutchinson, The Man and his Books,* Robert Green, Scarecrow Author Bibliographies, No. 70, Scarecrow Press, 1985. This includes a full index of textual material held in The Humanities Research Center, University of Texas at Austin, but is a difficult volume to obtain except in research libraries. HRC is used as an abbreviation here for The Humanities Research Center.

The Novels

Dates are of first English publication and publisher.

Thou Hast A Devil, 1930. Ernest Benn. (Virtually unobtainable except in research libraries.)
The Answering Glory, 1932. Cassell.
The Unforgotten Prisoner, 1933. Cassell.
One Light Burning, 1935. Cassell.
Shining Scabbard, 1936. Cassell.
Testament, 1938. Cassell.
The Fire and the Wood, 1940. Cassell.
Interim, 1945. Cassell.
Elephant and Castle, 1949. Cassell.
Recollection of a Journey, 1952. Cassell. (Published in the United States as *Journey With Strangers,* 1952. Rinehart.)
The Stepmother, 1955. Cassell.
March the Ninth, 1957. Geoffrey Bles.
Image of My Father, 1961. Geoffrey Bles. (Published in the United States as *The Inheritor,* 1962. Harper & Bros.)

A Child Possessed, 1964. Geoffrey Bles.
Johanna at Daybreak, 1969. Michael Joseph.
Origins of Cathleen, 1971. Michael Joseph.
Rising, 1976. Michael Joseph.

Unpublished Novels

'The Hand of the Purple Idol'. Schoolboy novel held in the
    HRC.
'The Caravan of Culture'. Held in the HRC.

Short Stories

There were 28 stories published in a variety of journals. A collection
of 22 of these was published in *The Quixotes and Other Stories: The
Selected Short Stories of R.C. Hutchinson*. ed. Robert Green, Carcanet
Press, 1984. Four newly published stories were included. The six
remaining published stories are:

'The Everyday Weekend'. *Punch*, May 1936.
'Go Between'. *News Chronicle*, September 1936.
'Education in Blackmail'. *News Chronicle*, February 1937.
'Siesta'. Read by R.C.H. on the British Broadcasting
    Corporation's National Programme, August 1939.
'Old English Custom'. *Evening News*, September 1953.
'Woman of Simplicity'. *She*, February 1956.

There are 23 stories that remain unpublished and these can be found
in the HRC collection.

Plays

Last Train South, Produced at St Martin's Theatre,
    Shaftesbury Avenue, London, August to
    September 1938. The typescript is at the HRC.

There are nine unpublished plays in manuscript at H.R.C. An adaptation
of *The Stepmother* by Warren Chetham-Stroude was published by
Samuel French, London, 1959.

Unperformed Adaptations of Novels

> Script for three-act television adaptation of *March the Ninth* by Elizabeth Lincoln, 1961. The typescript is in the HRC, while a Twentieth Century Fox film option was taken out in 1957.
> Neil Paterson wrote a script for adaptation of *The Stepmother* for Paramount in 1961.
> Guy Green produced *Stephan's Child,* a screenplay adaptation of *A Child Possessed,* which can be found in the HRC.

Diary

R.C.H.'s diary kept as a schoolboy is held in the HRC.

Military History

> *Paiforce: The Official Story of the Persia and Iraq Command, 1941-1946.* His Majesty's Stationary Office, London, 1949.
> Letter from R.C.H. to *The Times* concerning Paiforce, 19 March 1946.

Letters

There are over 270 entries in the catalogue at the HRC listing collections and individual letters from and to R.C.H. involving dozens of correspondents.

> *Two Men of Letters: Correspondence between R.C. Hutchinson Novelist and Martyn Skinner Poet, 1957-1974.* ed. Rupert Hart-Davis. Michael Joseph, London, 1979. The originals of the correspondence are held in the Bodleian Library, Oxford. Obtained in 1972.

Notebooks

Several boxes of notebooks containing drafts of novels and articles are held in the HRC.

R.C.H. on Ernest Raymond

Essay on Ernest Raymond, *Camden Journal*,
    December 1968.
'Ernest Raymond', Obituary, Royal Society of Literature
    Reports for 1973-75.

R.C.H. Broadcasts and Articles on Novel Writing

'Unfinished Novel', Talk on British Broadcasting
    Corporation's Home Service, October 1956 (extracts
    read by Carleton Hobbes).
'My Apologia', *John O'London's Weekly*, April 1949. Also
    published as 'If One Must Write Fiction', *The Saturday
    Review of Literature*, September 1949.
'My First Novel', *The Listener*, April 1953.
'The Pace for Living', *The Listener*, September 1953.

General Studies of R.C.H.'s Writing

'Birth of *A Child Possessed*', *Mental Health*, Spring 1962.
Anon., Obituary, *The Times*, 5 July 1975.
Rupert Hart-Davis, Obituary, *The Times*, 9 July 1962.
Derek Severn, 'R.C. Hutchinson: A Neglected Genius',
    Broadcast, British Broadcasting Corporation Radio
    Three, 4 September 1976; reprinted as 'The Hutchinson
    Question' in *The Listener*, 9 September 1976.
Mervyn Horder, 'One Light Burning: The World of R.C.
    Hutchinson', *London Magazine*, December 1977.
Robert Green, 'The Novels of R.C. Hutchinson', *English
    Studies in Africa*, March 1983.
Valentine Cunningham, 'Hauntings and Holocaust',
    The Times Literary Supplement, 23 September 1983.
Robert Green, '*Paiforce*: The Novelist as Military
    Historian', *Army Quarterly and Defence Journal*,
    April 1985.
Bishop Richard Harries, 'Thought for the Day', British
    Broadcasting Corporation Radio 4, 4 July 1986 (based
    on *Johanna at Daybreak*).

Bishop Richard Harries, *After the Evil: Christianity and Judaism in the Shadow of the Holocaust*. Passage on *Johanna at Daybreak*. Oxford University Press, 2003.

J.C. ('Jonty') Driver, 'Living in Interesting Times: On the Novels of R.C. Hutchinson', *Slightly Foxed*, issue 35, September 2012.

Index

You may also be interested in:

Richard Aldington

Vivien Whelpton

The story of Richard Aldington, outstanding Imagist poet and author of the bestselling war novel Death of a Hero (1929), takes place against the backdrop of some of the most turbulent and creative years of the twentieth century.

Vivien Whelpton provides a remarkably detailed and sensitive portrayal of the writer from the age of thirty-eight to his death from a heart attack in 1962. The first volume, *Richard Aldington: Poet, Soldier and Lover 1911-1929*, described Aldington's life as a stalwart of the pre-war London literary scene, his experience as an infantryman on the Western Front and his postwar personal and creative crises; this second volume seeks to balance the stories of Aldington's subsequent public and private lives through a careful reading of his novels, poems and letters with his circle of acquaintances.

The ways in which Aldington's dysfunctional childhood and survivor's guilt continued to haunt him through the inter-war years and beyond are masterfully untangled by an author with gifted psychological insight into her subject. This authoritative biography recounts the life of one of the most underrated writers of the last century.

Vivien Whelpton is a former teacher of English and Media Studies with a special interest in the literature of the First World War. She has written journal articles and monographs in this field. She has an M.A. in War Studies and has conducted tours of the Western Front for several years. Her first volume, *Richard Aldington: Poet, Soldier and Lover* (The Lutterworth Press, 2014), was shortlisted for The Biographers' Club Tony Lothian Prize in 2011.

Published 2019

Volume 1

Paperback ISBN: 978 0 7188 9546 4

Volume 2

Paperback ISBN: 978 0 7188 9477 1

You may also be interested in:

A Time and a Place

George Crabbe, Aldeburgh and Suffolk

Frances Gibb

George Crabbe, eighteenth-century poet, clergyman and surgeon-apothecary, is best known for 'Peter Grimes', the tale of a sadistic fisherman that inspired Benjamin Britten's opera of the same name. The brutal crimes and 'tortur'd guilt' of Grimes play out within the bleak, improbably beautiful setting of Aldeburgh. While Crabbe has fallen in and out of fashion, the Suffolk town and its landscape have continued to captivate writers and artists, including Britten, Ronald Blythe, Susan Hill and Maggi Hambling – all drawn to the stark coastline, eerie mudflats and open skies.

In *A Time and a Place*, Frances Gibb engages afresh with Crabbe's writing – tracing, for the first time, the resonance of this place in his life and work. She delves into his creative struggles, religious faith, romantic loves and opium addiction. Above all, she explores the continual lure – for Crabbe and those who have followed – of the 'little venal borough', and the land and sea beyond.

Frances Gibb is an award-winning journalist and former Legal Editor of The Times. She contributes to publications including *The Times* and *Sunday Times, The Daily Telegraph* and *The Spectator*, as well as to national radio. She read English at the University of East Anglia and has an honorary masters degree from the Open University. Her family has been connected with Aldeburgh and Suffolk for more than fifty years.

Published 2022

Paperback ISBN: 978 0 7188 9611 9
ePub ISBN: 978 0 7188 9613 3
PDF ISBN: 978 0 7188 9612 6

You may also be interested in:

Arthur Mee

A Biography

Keith Crawford

Arthur Mee (1875-1943), best remembered as the creator of *The Children's Encyclopaedia*, was more than a popular editor, journalist and travel writer; for a generation of young readers and their parents, the name Arthur Mee truly meant something. For many in his audience, the narratives and discourses embedded within his writing tied together and legitimised a trinity of beliefs that lay at the heart of his nonconformist faith and character: God, England and Empire.

Despite the enormous appeal of his many published works, which during the first half of the twentieth century saw him become a household name and a major publishing brand, Mee has remained an ethereal figure. In *Arthur Mee*, the first full-length account of Mee's life since 1946, Crawford draws upon a range of Mee's correspondence to offer for the first time a realistic picture of the man at work and at home as an antidote to the overly romanticised image attached to his name. The book places Mee's work within the wider cultural, political and social context of an England undergoing unparalleled societal change and technological advancement. Scholars of the history of education, children's literature and beyond will find much of interest in these pages, and childhood devotees to Mee's publications may well find themselves transported back to a time of wonder, imagination and hope.

Keith Crawford (PhD) is Adjunct Professor of Education in the School of Education at Macquarie University, Sydney. His current research focusses upon the social construction of national identity mediated through school history, geography and civic textbooks, school magazines and newspapers in Australia and the UK.

Published 2016
Paperback ISBN: 978 0 7188 9435 1
ePub ISBN: 978 0 7188 4462 2

C.S. Lewis at Poets' Corner

Edited by Michael Ward and Peter S. Williams

On the fiftieth anniversary of his death, C.S. Lewis was commemorated in Poets' Corner, Westminster Abbey, taking his place beside the greatest names in English literature. Oxford and Cambridge Universities, where Lewis taught, also held celebrations of his life. This volume gathers together addresses from those events into a single anthology.

Rowan Williams and Alister McGrath assess Lewis's legacy in theology, Malcolm Guite addresses his integration of reason and imagination, William Lane Craig takes a philosophical perspective, while Lewis's successor as Professor of Medieval and Renaissance English, Helen Cooper, considers him as a critic. Others contribute their more personal and creative responses: Walter Hooper, Lewis's biographer, recalls their first meeting; there are poems, essays, a panel discussion, and even a report by the famous "Mystery Worshipper" from the Ship of Fools website, along with a moving recollection by Royal Wedding composer Paul Mealor about how he set one of Lewis's poems to music. Containing theology, literary criticism, poetry, memoir, and much else, this volume reflects the breadth of Lewis's interests and the astonishing variety of his own output: a diverse and colourful commemoration of an extraordinary man.

Michael Ward is a Fellow of Blackfriars Hall, University of Oxford, and Professor of Apologetics at Houston Baptist University, Texas. He is author of *Planet Narnia: The Seven Heavens in the Imagination of C.S. Lewis* (2008).

Peter S. Williams is Assistant Professor in Communication and Worldviews at NLA University, Norway. His books include *C.S. Lewis vs. the New Atheists* (2013) and *A Faithful Guide to Philosophy* (2013).

Published 2017

Paperback ISBN: 978 0 7188 9485 6
PDF ISBN: 978 0 7188 4577 3

BV - #0002 - 091224 - C0 - 229/152/11 - CC - 9780718898007 - Matt Lamination